Julie Andrews

Julie

Andrews

James Arntz

and

Thomas S. Wilson

CONTEMPORARY BOOKS

A TRIBUNE NEW MEDIA/EDUCATION COMPANY

Library of Congress Cataloging-in-Publication Data

Arntz, James.
    Julie Andrews / James Arntz and Thomas S. Wilson.
        p.   cm.
    ISBN 0-8092-3267-7
    1. Andrews, Julie.   2. Motion picture actors and actresses—Great
Britain—Biography.   3. Singers—Great Britain—Biography.
I. Wilson, Thomas S.   II. Title.
PN2598.A65A87   1995
791.43'028'092—dc20
    [B]   95-38938
                                                  CIP

Cover and interior designs by Hespenheide Design
Back cover photos courtesy of the Academy of Motion Picture
Arts and Sciences, *Globe*, and Billy Rose Theatre Collection,
The New York Public Library for the Performing Arts, Astor,
Lenox, Tilden Foundation.

Published by Contemporary Books, Inc.
Two Prudential Plaza, Chicago, Illinois 60601-6790
Manufactured in the United States of America
International Standard Book Number: 0-8092-3267-7
10   9   8   7   6   5   4   3   2   1

Contents

Foreword by Carol Burnett

Julie Andrews . . . I first met my chum face to face in 1960 when a mutual friend brought her to see me in the off-Broadway musical *Once upon a Mattress*. He was sure we'd "hit it off."

Actually, I had seen Julie in *My Fair Lady* a few years before that, when I was the lucky recipient of the winning number for a pair of tickets donated to the Rehearsal Club, where I was living at the time. (The Rehearsal Club provided "a home for young ladies interested in the theater"—$18 a week, room and board. The famous play and movie *Stage Door* was written about this terrific boarding house.) I was thrilled to have the tickets to *My Fair Lady,* which was the biggest hit on Broadway. And Julie Andrews turned out to be the most wonderful leading lady I had ever seen. I also spotted her once on the street even earlier, when she was the toast of the town doing *The Boy*

Friend. As I walked past her, I realized who she was and turned around. She had dark hair and the whitest skin I had ever seen. Snow White immediately came to mind.

So . . . here I was, backstage after *Mattress,* shaking hands with Julie Andrews. Our mutual friend took us to a Chinese restaurant for a late supper, but once we'd ordered, he never got a word in. She and I chatted, guffawed, and dished until our chopsticks were confiscated by a tired waiter who wanted to go home. We had, indeed, "hit it off." She was "London" and I was "San Antone" . . . and we clicked. We clicked (as Julie puts it) as "chums."

After that mooshoo–gaipan evening, Julie appeared as a guest on the weekly CBS television program "The Garry Moore Show," on which I was a regular. We performed a finale which brought the audience to its feet—"Big D," from

the Broadway musical *The Most Happy Fella*. We were dressed as two tough "cowboys" who hit it off when we discovered that we were both from Dallas . . . a bit of a stretch for Julie, but she tackled it without a qualm and pulled it off without a hitch.

It was one of those rare moments where synergy happens. We weren't really surprised; it had already occurred when we were on our second egg roll the night we met. But as far as "show business" was concerned, we made an impression, and we were off and running. "Big D" led to our first television special: "Julie and Carol at Carnegie Hall." Taped in March of 1962, it was the first American TV show to be awarded the Montreaux Golden Rose Award.

Our paths separated then. Julie went on to the big screen; I stayed with the little one. Though we kept in touch, we rarely found chances to get together. We each had our families and separate careers. Finally, nine years later, we joined forces professionally for our second CBS special, "Julie and Carol at Lincoln Center." The premise was "What on *earth* have you been *doing* these past ten years?" Julie said the line brilliantly, and it got a great laugh. God, it was fun working with her again! It felt as if we had never been apart.

Years passed . . . but the feelings were still there, and we got together in 1989 for a third television special ("Julie and Carol Together Again"), performed at the Pantages Theater in Hollywood. There we were backstage, waiting for the downbeat of the overture, holding each other's sweaty hands and giggling nervously at what lay ahead. The twenty-seven years since Carnegie Hall seemed but an eyeblink.

But for some reason, this third show was having "backstage problems"—not between Julie and me, but some other ego-busting stuff was going on, and I was letting it get to me. In other words, I was pissed off, and it was eating at me. The overture began, the audience was waiting to see how these two broads were going to look, sound, and perform after all those years, and there I was thinking and roiling about "backstage intrigue." Julie saw the state I was in and took my hand, looked me in the eye, and said (and I know I'm paraphrasing):

> Chum, let's just go out there and have ourselves a ball. That's what we owe ourselves and the audience. Forget about any and all "crap"! We're here to have fun, and we're here for each other. Otherwise we wouldn't be doing this, would we?

That did it. With her words, I was able to let it all go. We hugged and went out to greet a warm, wonderful audience that rose to its feet. All the years vanished, and there we were, my chum and I, kicking up our heels, belting out songs, doing pratfalls, and generally enjoying the pleasure of making fools of ourselves in front of a welcoming bunch of people.

We're still in touch. I'm back in New York rehearsing a Broadway show—my first in thirty years. Just yesterday, a note from Julie finally tracked me down here at the hotel. She had sent it from Chicago, where she was previewing *Victor/Victoria*, her own return to Broadway after three decades. In the note, she said she had a dream about *us*, "a complicated scenario, but it had to do with the fact of the two of us coming back to Broadway this fall." She wrote other things and sent me her love—and Blake's. It was lovingly signed "Jools."

Ah, Jools, there couldn't be anything more fun than the two of us in town at the same time, doing our Broadway shows . . . unless, someday, it can be the two of us performing together again, one more time! I love you, Julie.

Carol

P.S. To whomever reads this: Julie Andrews is nothing like Snow White . . . or Mary Poppins either. She's a bawdy yet classy dame! Period.

1
Early Stages

Julia Elizabeth Wells was born October 1, 1935, in Walton-on-Thames, a suburb just south of London. Her father, Ted Wells, was a schoolteacher; her mother, Barbara, an accomplished pianist. Barbara gave piano lessons to the local children and served as accompanist in a small dancing school run by her sister, Joan Morris. From a very early age, baby Julia was aware of the sound of music. As a toddler, she was already learning tap and ballet from her Aunt Joan, and her mother recalled Julie's singing "Alice Blue Gown" in a "sweet little piping treble."

By the time she was three years old, Julie had learned to read and write from her father, who disapproved of traditional educational regimens. Ted Wells chose to provide most of his daughter's early education outside of the school system, and Julie displayed such exceptional imagination, intelligence, and musical talent that both parents became convinced she would find success in the world of entertainment.

In the summer of 1939, when Julie was almost four, Barbara secured a position as pianist for a music hall theater in the coastal resort town of Bognor Regis. One of the featured performers was Ted Andrews, a burly tenor billed as "The Canadian Troubadour." At the end of the season, Ted and Barbara became a vaudeville team. In the early stages of the war, while Julie and her younger brother John were evacuated to a riding school in Kent, the Canadian Troubadour and his new accompanist toured Britain, performing for the armed services. The relationship between Barbara and Ted Wells quickly deteriorated. When Julie was

four, her parents divorced, Barbara married Ted Andrews, and the newlyweds moved with Julie to North London.

Ted began giving singing lessons to Julie, partly to keep her occupied during the wartime disruptions, partly in an effort to ingratiate himself with her, partly to satisfy his new wife's ambitions for her daughter. On occasion, he and Barbara incorporated Julie into their music hall act—Ted would lift her onto a beer crate near the microphone, and the two would sing a sentimental duet while Barbara accompanied them on the piano. Theater managers liked the family act, and eventually Julie changed her last name to Andrews to make the billing simpler.

When Julie was seven, Ted Andrews took her to Leeds to audition for a world-famous singing teacher, Lillian Stiles-Allen. Madame Stiles-Allen was impressed by the child's phenomenal range, but she was also concerned that serious voice training might do lasting damage to Julie's young vocal chords. Julie was subsequently sent to throat specialists, who discovered that she had a fully developed adult larynx. This explained her "freak" four-octave range, from two C's above middle C to two C's below. The doctors concluded that singing lessons would do Julie no harm.

Thus, at age eight, Julie began a serious program of study with Madame Stiles-Allen, traveling alone on the two-hundred-mile train journey from London to Leeds and spending at least four days per week with her teacher. She came to love both Lillian Stiles-Allen and the lessons, which frequently ranged beyond music to metaphysical questions about life and art. Stiles-Allen stressed the responsibility of an artist to her audience. She was also a stickler for diction: "I always made a point with Julie that singing is musical speech. They are not two things apart. Bring the voice forward, use the words, fill the words, diction!"

With Madame Stiles-Allen's guidance, Julie's four-octave range developed into an astonishing musical instrument, and "Little Julie Andrews" soon became a popular child performer in England. She spent much of her childhood either studying voice or touring the music halls with her mother and stepfather. The family moved a number of times during those years, and it was rather a lonely life for Julie. By the end of the war, the Andrews family had finally settled permanently in Walton-on-Thames, Julie's birthplace, in a large shingled cottage called "The Old Meuse."

The property included a huge garden, and for several months, Julie enjoyed a relatively normal childhood, climbing trees and playing games with her two young half-brothers and their neighborhood friends. However, once Julie turned twelve, she became exempt from a regulation barring children from appearing on the London stage, and she was immediately cast in a new West End revue called *Starlight Roof*. On opening night, October 23, 1947, little Julie stopped the show. She became a star that night, and she has been working—and thrilling audiences—ever since.

Julia Wells, age three, with her younger brother, John. Her mother recalled that Julie "lived in a world peopled with fabulous story- *book characters. We always kept a prop box with a host of stage clothes and accessories. It was Julie's paradise."*

Julia and her nanny, Ethel Buchanan, on the pier at Bognor Regis.

The Wells family on the beach at Bognor Regis during the fateful summer of 1939: (from left) Julie's little brother John, father Ted, mother Barbara, aunt Joan Morris, and Pat, another nanny. Though Ted Wells won custody of both children after the divorce, he made the painful decision to send Julie to live with her mother. He felt the little girl needed a mother's care. Barbara had also persuaded him that she could best forward Julie's stage career.

Julie, at age eleven, singing with Ted Andrews. Her mother Barbara accompanies them. At first, Julie hated the lessons and practice, and she particularly resented her stepfather. Ultimately, she learned to love performing and grew closer to her stepfather, whom she called "Pop" (her real father was always "Dad").

A publicity photo for the Andrews family vaudeville act. Julie made her first radio broadcast in 1946, singing a duet with Ted Andrews on a BBC variety show called "Monday Night at Eight."

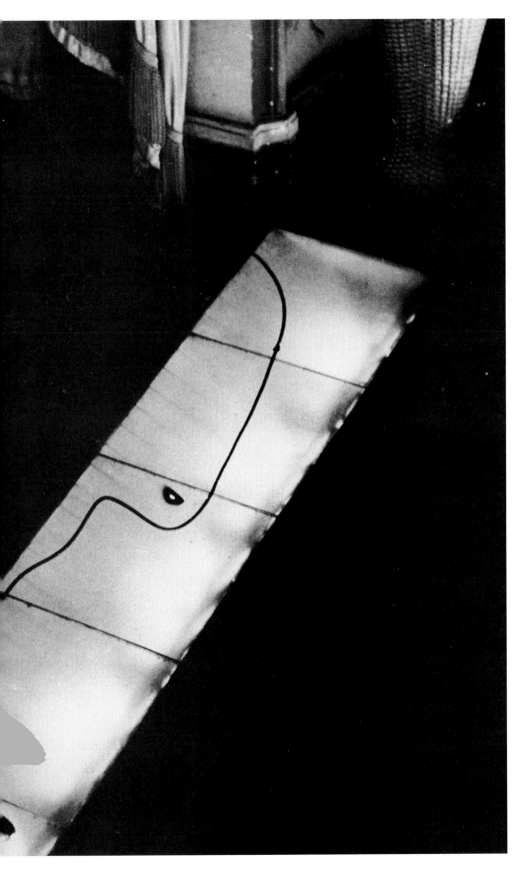

On December 5, 1946, Julie performed alone for the first time in a royal command performance at London's Stage Door Canteen. The Queen (now Queen Mother Elizabeth) and Princess Margaret were in attendance. In the receiving line after the show, the Queen told Julie that she "sang beautifully" and that she and the princess had "enjoyed it very much."

The Andrews family on holiday in Blackpool. Julie loved looking after her two young half-brothers, Christopher and Donald, who remember her as a kind of mini–Mary Poppins.

A carefree moment at the family home in Walton-on-Thames (opposite).

An "at-home" publicity photo with half-brother Donald. In the years immediately after the war, Julie's mother and step-father began a concerted effort to build name recognition both for Julie as an individual and for the Andrews family act.

In 1947 Julie made her professional stage debut at the London Hippodrome in a new musical revue called Starlight Roof. She entered the back of the audience during the first-act comedy routine of Wally Boag (right), who told jokes while he shaped balloons into animal forms. When Boag offered the balloons to children in the audience, Julie would run up the aisle asking for a balloon. Vic Oliver (left), the host of the show, then invited her onto the stage, where he engaged her in banter and finally asked her to sing something. The twelve-year-old would sing a famous soprano aria, the "Polonaise" from Mignon, in which she soared to an awesome F above high C. Audiences were stunned by the performance of this little girl in pigtails and party dress, and the show became a smash hit.

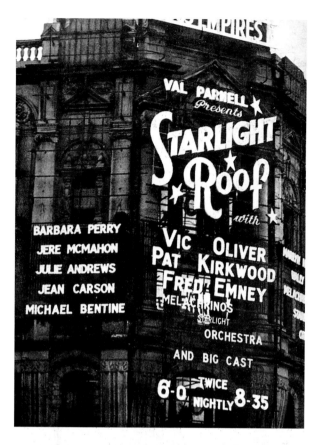

Julie appeared twice
nightly in Starlight Roof
until October 1948, when
she had to leave because a
regulation prohibited
minors from performing in
a show for more than one
year. The London County
Council also forbade any
performer under fifteen to
be in a theater after ten
o'clock at night, so Julie
was never allowed to take
part in the curtain calls.
Strict rules also governed a
child performer's studies.
Here, a couple of weeks
after her thirteenth birthday, Julie posed backstage
with her homework.

Booking cards were sub-
mitted to talent agents by
the owners or managers
of music hall theaters
around the country. The
reports about Julie were
almost always effusive,
but some of the bookers
considered the Ted and
Barbara Andrews act
old-fashioned.

METRO-GOLDWYN-MAYER BRITISH STUDIOS LTP
TEST OF
JULIE ANDREWS

HEIGHT	WEIGHT	AGE	EXPERIENCE
4'10½"	79 lbs.	12	STAGE AND RADIO

DIRECT RECORDING

DIRECTOR .... PAT JACKSON
CAMERAMAN .... BUNNY FRANCKE
DATE DECEMBER 1947

In 1947 Julie made a screen test for the British division of MGM. With her mother at the piano, she sang in a rather plain Margaret O'Brien–style outfit; then they dolled her up in ribbons and curls for a question-and-answer session. Julie was somewhat ill at ease in the test; the studio decided not to sign her. Rumors that she was unsuitable for film haunted her career for years after.

"England's Juvenile Singing Sensation" (as she was billed in those days) seeking an autograph from Danny Kaye. Kaye was the headliner, and Julie was on the bill, for a Royal Command Variety Performance at the London Palladium, November 1, 1948. She almost missed out on this very important engagement because she'd been instructed by her mother never to open notes and letters received from fans. Barbara Andrews preferred to screen her daughter's mail, in case there was anything "inappropriate." As a result, Julie had stashed the royal invitation in her coat pocket and remembered it only hours before the deadline for acceptance. She was the youngest solo performer ever to be seen in a Royal Command Variety Performance.

Programme continued

(The Pace Changes)

JULIE ANDREWS

Our Youngest
Operatic Soprano

Julie's program listing for the Royal Command Variety Performance. She watched the cream of British variety performers that night and especially enjoyed the legendary male impersonator Ella Shields, who sang "Burlington Bertie from Bow." The song was to become a standard in Julie's adult career.

Julie was ninth on the bill at the Royal Command Variety Performance. Once again, she sang the "Polonaise" from Mignon, *and once again she stopped the show. After leading the company in "God Save the King," she met King George VI, Queen Elizabeth, Prince Philip, and Princess Margaret.*

Thirteen-year-old Julie with Humpty, her new pet corgi. Humpty was famous for howling whenever she sang.

In December 1948 Julie became part of another grand English tradition, the Christmas pantomime, when she was cast as Humpty in the London Casino production of Humpty Dumpty. *Based on familiar fairy tales, the pantomimes are produced every year for limited runs during the Christmas season. The shows feature popular songs, sing-alongs, variety acts, and some unusual casting: the principal boy and girl are both played by girls, and the female character roles are filled by male comedians. Julie met young Tony Walton (later to be her first husband) after a performance of the show. Because his family also lived in Walton-on-Thames, the two teenagers became immediate friends.*

In 1950 Julie began appearing regularly on a very popular BBC radio show called "Educating Archie." Hosted by Peter Brough, the comedy show featured his dummy, Archie Andrews, as well as Max Bygraves and Benny Hill. Singing songs such as "The Blue Danube" and "The Gentle Lark," Julie had the weekly song spot and attracted bags of fan mail.

In another pantomime,
Red Riding Hood, *pro-
duced in Nottingham in
1950, Julie played the title
role, also identified as The
Baron's Ward. Whenever
Red Riding Hood was
frightened, she would
sing, giving Julie ample
opportunity to show her
stuff. Her repertoire
included "Rudolph the
Red-Nosed Reindeer,"
sung with the "principal
boy," actress Cherry Lind
(at right).*

Britain's *"Phenomenal
Young Vocal Star" cele-
brates her fifteenth birthday at the* BBC's *Paris
Casino studio. She is
quoted as proclaiming,
"At last I am free from the
London County
Council!" The Council
had strictly governed her
education and work
hours, and the young per-
former was eager to begin
setting her own rules.*

On October 8, 1949, Julie appeared in a BBC television program called "Radiolympia Showtime." Julie was becoming increasingly uncomfortable with her little-girl image: "Most of the time, I was kept in short, short dresses, patent-leather shoes, and ankle socks, trying desperately to look ten years younger than I really was." Others in the cast that night were singer Vera Lynn and music hall comedian Stanley Holloway, who was to play Julie's father in My Fair Lady.

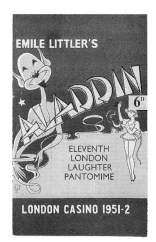

Julie was back at the London Casino in 1951 for the Christmas pantomime Aladdin. *On these two pages she is seen as Princess Balroulbadour. Aladdin is played by actress Jean (Jeannie) Carson, who later emigrated to America and was seen in a number of early television shows, including her own series, "Hey Jeannie!"*

Aladdin *closed in February 1952, but Julie had no concerns about employment. She was already cast in a touring revue called* Look In; *in May she joined Ted and Barbara Andrews in a variety show at the Victoria Palace in London (Joan Collins and Sophie* Tucker *were also on the bill); she was featured in a* BBC *radio series, "Here Comes the Pleasure Boat"; and she ended the year at the Coventry Hippodrome playing Princess Bettina in another Christmas pantomime,* Jack and the Beanstalk. *Her weekly* salary *for the latter was £250, a record for a performer her age. Julie Andrews was hot; Ted and Barbara Andrews were not; and that turn of events became a point of serious tension in the Andrews household.*

Julie's voice was used in an animated feature, The Rose of Baghdad, which was released in Britain in 1952. The cartoon was originally produced in Italy in 1949, then redubbed into English, with Julie as the voice of Princess Zeila. In yet another incarnation, the movie was retitled The Singing Princess and released in the United States in 1967 to capitalize on the grown-up Julie's screen popularity.

An insert from a British magazine from 1952. Although Julie was now sweet sixteen, the public still tended to think of her as a child. Like most child stars, she had a difficult time making the transition to more grown-up roles.

Julie's mother finally acknowledged reality and allowed Julie's manager, Charles Tucker, to place her under the tutelage of Pauline Grant, a ballet teacher who took charge not only of Julie's dance training but also of her appearance, attire, and deportment. Ted and Barbara Andrews faced another reality as well. Ted took a sales job, Barbara looked after the household, and Julie became the primary breadwinner in the family. This is one of the last photos to capture the "little Julie" image.

In 1953 Julie toured for three months in a revue called Cap and Belles, *singing as well as dancing with the elaborately costumed corps de ballet. The show played Brighton, Birmingham, and Glasgow. The press took note of a more grown-up Julie and were particularly impressed with her first off-the-shoulder dress (opposite page).*

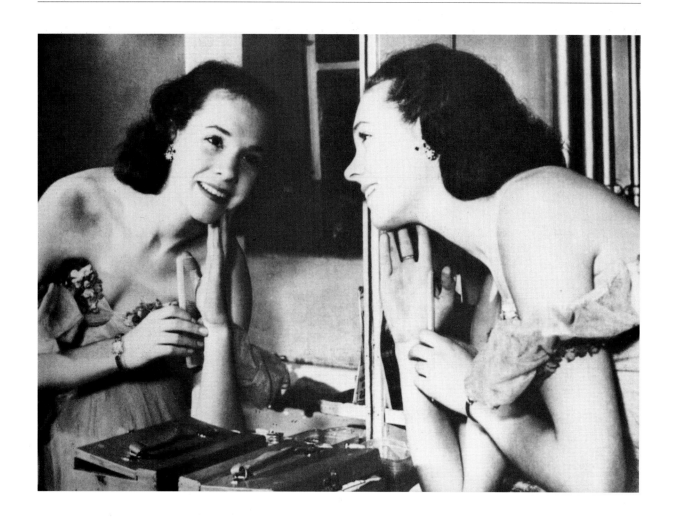

Julie was a frequent guest artist on British radio. Here she is seen rehearsing with Stanley Black's Concert Orchestra for a weekly broadcast called "Top of the Town."

For a BBC television program called "Puzzle Corner" (November 21, 1953), Julie's agent, Charles Tucker, printed up postcards to promote her appearance.

This 1953 publicity photo (opposite top) offers further evidence that stylist Pauline Grant was having a liberating effect not only on Julie's appearance but on her sense of self as well. British ladies' magazines began to feature Julie in articles on clothing and makeup tips.

On June 5, 1953, Julie sang for a BBC radio show with the Roy Terry Orchestra and the George Mitchell Mariners (opposite bottom). More than 3,700 people crowded the banks of Greenwich Pier to see the broadcast from the BBC Showboat, which had been created in celebration of coronation year.

CHARLES L. TUCKER

requests you to please look in this SATURDAY on your T.V. to see

JULIE ANDREWS

in **" PUZZLE CORNER "**

at 8.30 p.m.

When Julie was not on tour, her Aunt Joan would provide a private morning lesson in ballet and tap. Often, Julie also joined an evening class in ballroom dancing.

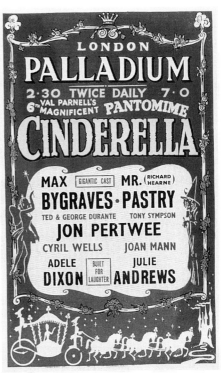

In December 1953 Julie played the title role in her final pantomime, Cinderella. *The evening included a broomstick ballet, live ponies, and the usual mix of comedy and popular songs. Cinderella was Julie's fifth Christmas pantomime and her greatest London success up to that time. She was eighteen and at a point in her career in which she was making a good living, receiving considerable public acclaim, enjoying an interesting circle of friends, and for the first time leading an independent life. In her own words, "I really thought that that would be it. I would just go round and round England and sing in pantomimes and vaudeville."*

During the run of Cinderella *Julie was seen by theater director Vida Hope and composer Sandy Wilson, who were casting a Broadway production of their London musical hit,* The Boy Friend. *Both felt that Julie possessed the innocence and poise they were seeking for Polly Browne, the lead ingenue in the show. They offered her a two-year contract, but Julie turned them down. After years of touring, the notion of travel always made her anxious, and she was also genuinely concerned about the welfare of her family.*

After Cinderella, *Julie appeared on* BBC *Television singing "Berkeley Square" on a program called "Limelight" (July 26, 1954) and made her debut as a dramatic actress in a new play,* Mountain Fire, *at the Liverpool Court Theatre. She played a winsome Tennessee belle, Becky Dunbar, who is impregnated by a traveling salesman (portrayed by American actor Jerry Wayne, right), then left to sing "Lullaby to an Unborn Child," one of three songs added to the play for Julie. Subplots included bootleg whiskey and the Ku Klux Klan. Julie recalls, "Happily, it never came to London; otherwise, I'd almost certainly have never worked again. You've never heard a worse Southern accent than mine." Actually, the out-of-town critics were quite complimentary about her performance.*

Julie made her first cabaret appearance during this period, but there were no other job offers on the horizon. There was renewed pressure from Cy Feuer, the American producer of The Boy Friend. Feuer had seen Julie in Mountain Fire *and agreed that she was ideal for his musical. Everyone in her life—friends, family, teachers, agent—insisted that Julie would be making a huge mistake if she passed up the chance to perform a leading role on Broadway. Finally, she discussed her dilemma with her father, Ted Wells, and he strongly encouraged her to seize this opportunity. Julie relented, but only for a one-year contract.*

The Broadway publicity machine thoroughly covered Julie's departure for New York. Here she is seen in her bedroom in Walton-on-Thames, laying out clothes for her trip to America. She takes a keepsake family photograph—from left, her half-brother Donald, Aunt Joan, half-brother Chris, her mother Barbara, and Humpty. Humpty appears again with Julie in the bay window of "The Old Meuse," her childhood home. The final photograph shows Julie with her Boy Friend costar, John Hewer, just before their departure for New York.

2
Broadway

The American producers of *The Boy Friend* had originally planned to bring the English cast of the show directly to Broadway during the 1955–56 season, after the hit show had settled into its London run. Luckily for Julie, another twenties-style show, a revival of *Good News*, was announced for Broadway, and the threat of competition persuaded the producers to open *The Boy Friend* sooner. The producers elected to cast a second company for Broadway and soon fell under the spell of eighteen-year-old Julie Andrews. After much persuasion, they convinced Julie to join the cast. She flew to New York on August 23, 1954.

During her first year in New York, Julie shared quarters with fellow cast member Dilys Laye, an exuberant, sociable young woman who helped allay Julie's frequent bouts of homesickness. *The Boy Friend* was a smash hit, and Julie was given featured billing, but she was still known to write long letters home detailing her adventures in America and yearning for her return to England at the end of the year's contract.

Gradually, she became more accustomed to the ways of the New World, and as the star of a successful Broadway show, she was quickly accepted into the vibrant theater community. Broadway was at its zenith in the mid-fifties, and the excitement was palpable. *Peter Pan*, *Damn Yankees*, and *The Pajama Game* were running concurrently with *The Boy Friend*, and *Bells Are Ringing*, *West Side Story*, *Gypsy*, *The Music Man*, *The Sound of Music*,

The ingenues of The Boy Friend, *all English girls on their first trip to the United States, were taken aback by the brashness of the New York press, which constantly hounded them for cheesecake shots. Here, in Times Square, the photographers were content with a more demure pose by cast members: (from left) Ann Wakefield, Stella Claire, Dilys Laye, Julie, and Millicent Martin.*

and *Bye Bye Birdie* were all about to appear on the scene.

As Julie's one-year contract was coming to a close, a representative of Alan Jay Lerner and Frederick Loewe asked Julie to audition for their musical adaptation of George Bernard Shaw's *Pygmalion.* She had just auditioned for *Pipe Dream*, a new Rodgers and Hammerstein production, but when Richard Rodgers learned that she was also under consideration for *My Fair Lady*, he advised her to take the other show if it was offered to her. Rodgers sensed that Julie would be perfect for the role of Eliza Doolittle. He also knew that *Pipe Dream* would do little for her career.

My Fair Lady became the hit of the decade, and Julie received a Tony Award nomination for her performance (Judy Holliday won the award that year for *Bells Are Ringing*). Julie played Eliza Doolittle for two years on Broadway and another sixteen months in London. During the latter run she married her childhood sweetheart, Tony Walton.

In the meantime, Lerner and Loewe were already preparing a new role for Julie in their musical *Camelot.* Her performance as Queen Guenevere garnered yet another Tony nomination, lost this time to Elizabeth Seal in *Irma La Douce.* Julie appeared in *Camelot* for almost two years before leaving in 1962 to have a baby. Just prior to her departure, she met with Walt Disney, who offered her a choice role in what was to be her first motion picture, *Mary Poppins.* Once Hollywood beckoned, Julie would not return to the stage for more than three decades.

Julie (third from the left) vamps with English director Vida Hope (at Julie's right). Choreographer John Heawood (far right) *put the girls through their paces. Julie described* The Boy Friend *as a "piece of lace."*

THE BOY FRIEND

Sandy Wilson's The Boy Friend *was a charming pastiche of the silly plots and infectious scores of musical comedy in the 1920s. Julie played Polly Browne, a wealthy young lady attending a posh finishing school somewhere along the Riviera. The plot revolved around Polly's confusion and uncertainty, first at not having a beau, and then at falling in love with a poor messenger boy.*

During rehearsals, composer Sandy Wilson and director Vida Hope became unhappy with the quicker pacing, larger orchestrations, and exaggerated tone of the Broadway production. They were eventually barred from the theater by producer Cy Feuer, who took over direction of the show. On the final night of previews, when Julie was floundering, he gave her some very valuable advice: "Everybody else is being funny. I want you to be absolutely straight, to be Polly Browne, to be that girl whose heart is breaking. If you do that, you could be a big star tomorrow night."

On opening night at the Royale Theatre, on September 30, 1954, Julie followed Feuer's instructions to the letter. Her trembling lower lip and demure, downcast eyes immediately endeared her to audience and critics alike. On the following day, Julie's nineteenth birthday, she and the show received rave

reviews; a short time later, her name went up on the theater marquee. She also received both the Donaldson Award and the Theatre World Award for this auspicious Broadway debut.

Though the masquerade ball song "Poor Little Pirouette" (above) was originally intended to be sung to Polly by the head-mistress (Ruth Altman), the director added Julie to the musical mix to capitalize on her special talent for soprano acrobatics.

The second act opened with a scene at the beach (right). Polly, troubled by her attraction to an "unsuitable" boy, stands deep in thought as her classmates frolic in their "bathing costumes." The five "perfect young ladies" in search of good manners and well-to-do beaux were the lively focus of this popular musical comedy, which launched Julie's Broadway career.

Polly and Tony (John Hewer) dream of a perfect life together in "A Room in Bloomsbury." The sweet moment is interrupted when Tony is mistaken for a jewel thief. Later, his true identity as the son of a millionaire brings the show to its happy ending. Julie recalls that during curtain calls, the audience was often on its feet and dancing the Charleston in the aisles.

Julie and Dilys Laye in their dressing room after opening night, with (from left) producer-director Cy Feuer, John Hewer, and coproducer Ernest Martin. Note the congratulatory telegrams on the wall.

Rehearsals for My Fair Lady *were particularly difficult both for Julie and for Rex Harrison. But because Harrison had no previous experience with musicals, he had received most of the attention from the show's creators. Finally, legendary theater director Moss Hart (left) noticed that Julie was having serious problems with the demanding role of Eliza Doolittle. He put aside a weekend, booked himself and Julie into the New Amsterdam Theatre, and devoted forty-eight hours entirely to her, going through the play line by line. Julie recalls, "Moss supplied the character, the route, and the direction; and as the weekend went by, I absorbed Eliza more and more." The following week at rehearsals, Rex Harrison remarked: "My word, you have improved."*

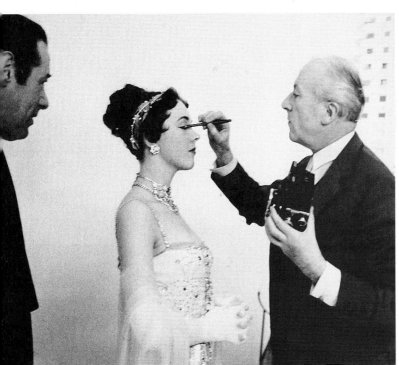

Another legend, English designer-photographer Cecil Beaton, created the grand Edwardian costumes for the show. Here he is touching up Julie's eyeliner for a publicity photograph. Julie recalls the elegant Beaton being in a fury as she exited the stage during the New Haven tryouts. Her wig was on backward. Yanking the wig, he exclaimed, "This way, you silly girl."

My Fair Lady

Many theater historians consider My Fair Lady *the crowning achievement of American musical theater. Based on George Bernard Shaw's great social comedy* Pygmalion, *and adapted by three titans of the theater—composer Frederick Loewe, lyricist Alan Jay Lerner, and playwright-director Moss Hart—the show is unquestionably a masterpiece of popular art. It also includes two of the most difficult and demanding roles in theater: the complex characters of Henry Higgins and Eliza Doolittle.*

About Eliza, Julie has said, "It's the greatest role that a woman can play in musical comedy, but it's such a huge piece. You have to scream like a cockney and then sing beautifully later on in the show. And then there are all the dramatic scenes. It's enormous." On another occasion, she noted, "It was in My Fair Lady *that I learned the business of the stage. I learned how to sustain a performance. It was marvelous discipline."*

After a rocky tryout period in New Haven and Philadelphia, My Fair Lady *finally opened in New York at the Mark Hellinger Theatre on March 15, 1956. It was an instant hit, an instant classic, and it catapulted Julie into a whole new category of international stardom. The songs from* My Fair Lady *dominated the airwaves, and Julie's*

lovely soprano became a familiar sound to virtually everyone in the English-speaking world.

Julie remained in the Broadway production of My Fair Lady *for two years, then opened the show in London, along*

with most of the key players from the original cast. Although some English critics fretted about an American rendering of Shaw, the Lerner and Loewe masterpiece was greatly anticipated in the West End. Opening night,

at the Theatre Royal Drury Lane, April 30, 1958, was a triumph.

Above, Julie as the spirited cockney flower girl, Eliza Doolittle.

Rex Harrison, Julie once said, was "magical on stage, and sometimes I'd find myself forgetting to be Eliza and just watch him with my mouth open." After her vocal breakthrough, having learned to pronounce her H's, Eliza, Colonel Pickering (Robert Coote), and Henry Higgins break into a triumphant tango, "The Rain in Spain." At the New Haven opening, the thunderous applause following this number literally stopped the show. Coote and Harrison sat stunned, but Julie, the veteran music hall performer, knew exactly what to do. "C'mon, boys," she said, and led the actors downstage for an impromptu bow.

During the tryout run in New Haven, Julie sang "Say a Prayer for Me Tonight" before departing for the Embassy Ball. The song was cut before the New York opening, and the writers used it later in their film Gigi. Julie has said, "It was my song, and I was sad when they cut it." There were compensations, however. In the photo above, she is seen introducing "I Could Have Danced All Night." A seemingly transformed Eliza (at left) tests her proper new persona on admirer Freddy (Michael King) and Henry Higgins's mother (Cathleen Nesbitt). However, the excitement of the "Ascot Gavotte" is too much for Eliza (over-leaf), and she urges her horse Dover to "move your bloomin' arse."

During the London run of My Fair Lady, *Julie posed backstage for Cecil Beaton in the new gown he had designed for her (opposite). Another Beaton gown (right) was created for the Embassy Ball, although the headdress was later simplified for the production. Beaton redesigned a number of costumes for the West End production, and women's fashions were heavily influenced by his interpretation of early twentieth-century English styles.*

Above, a wonderfully theatrical photograph of Julie in full stage makeup in her dressing room after opening night in London. She remained in the show until August 8, 1959. At the end of her final performance, the audience joined hands and sang "Auld Lang Syne." Julie left the stage in tears.

Director Moss Hart is
seen rehearsing Julie and
Richard Burton. "Camelot
was by far my favorite
show," Julie was quoted
as saying. "It had great
spirit, and I loved being
Guenevere." She also
appreciated a role that
demanded less energy and
allowed more time for
personal enjoyment both
on and off the stage.

The authors of My Fair Lady *were expected to deliver another spectacular hit with* Camelot, *particularly with the team of Julie Andrews and Richard Burton as Queen Guenevere and King Arthur. The box office advance climbed steadily to more than three million dollars, and Julie told reporters, "I'm one of the luckiest actresses alive, being able to work for the second time with the same wonderful team who created* My Fair Lady. *The score is the finest I've ever heard. I love every song."*

But the show seemed doomed when Moss Hart suffered a serious heart attack several days after the first preview in Toronto. Alan Jay Lerner had been ill as well and was released from the hospital the very day Hart was stricken. Costume designer Adrian had died shortly after the project was launched. Backers were understandably nervous about the show's prospects.

With Hart confined to his bed for the foreseeable future, Lerner took over the task of directing the production, cutting nearly an hour from the show during its second tryout period in Boston.

When Camelot *finally opened at the Majestic Theatre on December 3, 1960, the musical was still long, and critics were only partially pleased. They liked Julie, they loved the score, they raved about Richard Burton, and they*

enjoyed the lighthearted spirit of Act I. They also praised the show as one of the most lavish ever mounted. But about the dark second act, in which Camelot is destroyed by Guenevere's love for Lancelot, the press was less than enthusiastic.

Advance sales dropped perceptibly until "The Ed Sullivan Show" featured several minutes of the musical's pretty songs. The publicity attracted a new audience, and Moss Hart returned to cut another twenty minutes from the show. It seemed to make all the difference. Camelot enjoyed a very respectable run of 837 performances.

After the assassination of John F. Kennedy, the show became indelibly connected with the "brief shining moment" of his presidency.

In the production photo above, Guenevere prays to St. Genevieve to release her from the frightening prospect of marrying a man (King Arthur) she has never met. The song is "The Simple Joys of Maidenhood."

The creators of Camelot
with their handsome stars:
Richard Burton, Frederick
Loewe, Alan Jay Lerner,
and Julie Andrews.

When Arthur and Guenevere meet, he points out the many unique pleasures of his medieval kingdom in the famous title song, "Camelot." Julie recalls, "Richard would say to me, 'I will make the audience cry tonight with this speech, and in the same speech tomorrow night, I will make them laugh.' And he would do just that, and I would be awed." About Julie, Richard Burton was quoted as saying, "Every man I know who knows her is a little in love with her."

Camelot's most exemplary knight Sir Lancelot (Robert Goulet) visits the queen's bedchambers, where she confesses "I Loved You Once in Silence." This was Goulet's Broadway debut, and Julie vividly remembers the sexy sight of him in tights: "I used to sit offstage every night and watch him sing . . . and all I could think of was, 'Gee, the backs of his knees are just great!' His voice was pretty good too!"

In a boisterous celebration of spring, Guenevere and company sing "The Lusty Month of May." Julie has said that "there are occasions when an audience can really lift you. You find yourself singing your guts out for them. It's a current that passes from them to you and back." Such an occasion usually arose during this exuberant production number, which was a highlight of the show.

This opulent throne room in the grand hall offered a dazzling display of Arthurian pageantry. The elaborate costumes and sets prompted Broadway wags to dub the show "Costalot."

Legendary Hollywood designer Adrian created this sumptuous gown (opposite) for Queen Guenevere. After Adrian's death, the costumes were completed by Tony Duquette, who won a Tony Award for his fine work.

Under the red glow of dawn, Lancelot and Guenevere meet near the battlefield to ask forgiveness from King Arthur, whom they have betrayed by their love.

*Julie and Richard cele-
brate opening night. The
audience that night was
filled with celebrities,
among them Myrna Loy,
Burgess Meredith, Gloria
Swanson, and Marlene
Dietrich.*

*A candid shot (opposite)
of the queen of Broadway
sitting alone in the
Majestic Theatre during
her final year in* Camelot.
*Julie would not appear
again on Broadway for
thirty-three years.*

Camelot *was based on the
novel* The Once and
Future King *by T. H.
White. Here, White (at
left) greets first-nighter
Noel Coward at the open-
ing night party. Julie
became quite friendly with
White, who lived on
Alderney in the Channel
Islands. Sometime later
she and her husband,
Tony Walton, purchased a
cottage near White's ram-
bling estate.*

3
Movies

During the Broadway run of *Camelot*, Walt Disney made a special trip to New York to see the show. His studio was working on another Arthurian story, *The Sword in the Stone*, but Disney was also following a strong hunch that Julie Andrews would be perfect in the title role of his ambitious new live action movie musical. Julie's sharp, funny, commanding performance as Guenevere surpassed all of Disney's expectations. In a backstage visit after the show, he invited her to undertake her first film, *Mary Poppins*.

Julie delayed her response to Disney for as long as possible. Warner Brothers had yet to announce casting for the film version of *My Fair Lady*, and Julie still held some faint hope that the studio would break with Hollywood custom and offer her the plum role she had created on Broadway. When at last Jack Warner announced Audrey Hepburn for the role of Eliza Doolittle, Julie was disappointed but philosophical. She had created one of the great characters in the history of the Broadway musical, and it would have been "loverly" to make a permanent record of her performance.

But making *My Fair Lady* would have precluded her project with Disney, and both she and husband Tony Walton were charmed not only by Walt Disney, who personally toured them around Disneyland, but also by the script, storyboards, and score for *Mary Poppins*. Tony was engaged to design the costumes, and with a primarily English cast, they felt very much at home. Julie delayed no longer; she, Tony, and

their three-month-old daughter Emma moved to Hollywood.

Several months later, a proud, typically generous Walt Disney flouted the competitive customs of Hollywood and permitted a few of his competitors to screen some of Julie's scenes in *Mary Poppins*. The rumors that Julie was unphotogenic or "too stagey" for the movies were quickly put to rest.

In short order, producer Martin Ransohoff snapped her up for a dramatic role in *The Americanization of Emily* and Robert Wise cast her for a big-budget adaptation of Rodgers and Hammerstein's *The Sound of Music*. These old Hollywood pros were so confident of Julie's screen magic that all three films were completed, and millions of dollars invested, before the public's response to Julie would be tested with the release of *Mary Poppins* in the summer of 1964.

Julie's movie debut was the most spectacular in Hollywood history. *Mary Poppins* became Disney's highest grossing film, and *The*

Sound of Music (1965) still ranks among the all-time movie blockbusters. Even *The Americanization of Emily* (1964), a small, bittersweet, black-and-white comedy, managed to make money. The public *adored* Julie Andrews!

Indeed, her first six films were so successful that for nearly a decade Julie Andrews held the record as the highest grossing performer in the history of the movies. She also became an international media favorite, in constant demand for interviews and magazine covers.

Almost as abruptly, Julie's box office temperature plunged. It was partly the times—the countercultural late sixties were in full swing. Also, the films, though sumptuously produced and well performed, were somehow lacking the sunny persona so beloved by Julie's fans. Despite sensational musical numbers, *STAR!* (1968) was poorly received. *Darling Lili* (1970), Julie's first project with soon-to-be-second-husband Blake Edwards, became a notorious Hollywood flop. Movie offers were

dropped, and the fickle entertainment press turned sour, citing her reluctance to do interviews and the "goody-goody" image they had helped to create.

Julie and Blake actually left Hollywood for a time, and in the years after, she devoted far less time to a movie career. Most of her later films were made in collaboration with her writer-director husband. She had a secondary role in *"10"* (1979), which was an enormous success for Edwards, and they shared the laurels for their smash-hit musical farce, *Victor/Victoria* (1982).

With *S.O.B.* (1981), they directed a well-aimed jibe at both the movie business and Julie's chaste image. And in *That's Life* (1986), they improvised an effective, surprisingly intimate "home movie" about marital and family dynamics. Many feel that Julie's finest dramatic performance can be seen in *Duet for One* (1986), a thoughtful, beautifully crafted film by Andrei Konchalovsky about a concert violinist stricken with multiple sclerosis.

Like Julie, Dick Van Dyke considers himself a hoofer, not a dancer, and the two had a genuinely good time during the lengthy, often grueling musical rehearsals for Mary Poppins. He has called the film "the greatest experience of my life."

The imaginative "Jolly Holiday" segment was first filmed with the actors performing in front of a "sodium screen," which allowed cartoon characters and animation to be added to the scene later in the process. At the time of its release in 1964, Mary Poppins *featured state-of-the-art animation and received a special technical award from the Academy of Motion Picture Arts and Sciences.*

A rehearsal with composer-lyricist brothers Richard M. Sherman (at piano) and Robert B. Sherman (far right). Between Julie and Dick Van Dyke is musical arranger Irwin Kostal, whose association with Julie dated back to her earliest solo albums.

Walt Disney based Mary Poppins *on a popular series of children's books by Australian-English writer P. L. Travers. Travers was herself a formidable* Mary Poppins *type who personally called on Julie to assess her suitability for the "practically perfect" nanny with magical powers. Principal photography for the movie began in May 1963 and continued for nearly four months. The special effects would require another eleven months of painstaking work by Disney artists and technicians.*

Their efforts and Disney's vision were well rewarded. Advertised at the time as "Walt Disney's greatest achievement," Mary Poppins *was indeed his most acclaimed production. It was an enormous hit, earning an unprecedented $44 million in its first release. Since then, it has become a children's video favorite and will clearly endure as a family classic for decades to come.*

Julie and director Robert Stevenson (far left) pose with the distinguished British members of the Mary Poppins *cast: (left to right) Matthew Garber, Karen Dotrice, David Tomlinson, Glynis Johns, Arthur Treacher, Hermione Baddeley, and Elsa Lanchester. About working with Julie, Bob Stevenson said, "When she comes on stage, she always brings the sunshine with her."*

Julie's first husband, Tony Walton, created the charming costumes for Mary Poppins *and served as design consultant on* the film. It was the only time in their marriage that they were able to work together. Both conceded that her tremendous suc- cess in Hollywood, and his as a theater designer in London and New York, contributed to the failure of their marriage.

The unpredictable nanny
pops her charges into a
chalk pavement drawing
for the animated "Jolly
Holiday" fantasy.

(overleaf) "Step in Time,"
the chimney-sweep ballet
across the rooftops of
London, is one of the
most exhilarating musical
scenes in movie history.

Special effects fireworks
added to the color and
excitement, and as always,
Julie's poise and impeccable bearing held the focus
of this epic scene.

The world premiere of Mary Poppins *was scheduled at Grauman's Chinese Theatre in Hollywood on August 27, 1964. A very pleased Walt Disney joined his two stars for the grand celebration of his crowning achievement.*

Merchandising had become an increasingly important element in the promotional campaigns for Hollywood films, and toy stores were soon filled with Mary Poppins dolls, games, books, tea sets, and lunch boxes.

Mary Poppins *was nominated for thirteen Academy Awards and won five, including a Best Actress award for Julie Andrews. Ironically,* My Fair Lady *won most of the other major awards that year.*

THE AMERICANIZATION OF EMILY

The Americanization of Emily *was a distinct change of pace for Julie. Director Arthur Hiller detected strong dramatic instincts in Julie Andrews, and she confirmed his judgment with a very solid performance as Emily Barham, an English motor-pool driver who has lost her father, brother, and husband in the early years of World War II.*

Screenwriter Paddy Chayefsky (Marty, Network) wrote this antiwar love story about Emily's affair with U.S. Naval Commander Charlie Madison (James Garner), a pragmatist and self-proclaimed coward who ends up with the first wave of sailors on Omaha Beach. Both Julie and James Garner cite The Americanization of Emily *as one of their favorite films, and it is in fact a highlight of their careers.*

Even before Mary Poppins *was released, director Arthur Hiller was predicting that Julie "will be, if not number one, at least in the top five stars—and we all know it. It became clear to me about midway in the making of* Emily.*"*

Arthur Hiller is seated at left, rehearsing the famous tea party scene with Julie, Garner, and lovely English character actress Joyce Grenfell (back to camera), who plays Julie's disconsolate mother. Screenwriter Paddy Chayefsky looks on.

Julie recalls that in her first movie love scene "Jimmy Garner kissed divinely, take after take; and I thought, well, I'm going to be professional about this, and then I got up off the bed and promptly fell down. My knees simply buckled." She had less difficulty with the crisp Chayefsky dialogue, which was also very much against type: "You're a scoundrel, Charlie. I don't mind making love to a scoundrel, but I think it is immoral to marry one. . . . Oh, Lord, I hope I don't get pregnant."

A very glamorous portrait of Julie as Emily, who ultimately gives her heart to Charlie Madison because she has judged him the least likely man to see combat. Fate and the madness of war disrupt their happiness.

The poster art for Emily reflected the adult nature of the film but played down its seriocomic tone. By the mid-sixties, almost all Hollywood movies were being made in color. Director Hiller and producer Martin Ransohoff chose black-and-white film both to complement Chayefsky's message and to better integrate documentary footage of the D-Day invasion.

Julie and husband Tony Walton attended the premiere of The Americanization of Emily *in New York City's Loew's State Theater in the fall of 1964. The film and Julie's performance were both critically* acclaimed, but the picture was eclipsed by Mary Poppins *and* The Sound of Music. *At the time, very few took note of the fact that Julie was highly effective in a mature, passionate, nonmusical role.*

THE SOUND OF MUSIC

During the planning stages of The Sound of Music, legendary Hollywood wag Billy Wilder is reputed to have exclaimed, "No musical with swastikas in it will ever be a success." Mr. Wilder was wildly off the mark: The Sound of Music was not only a success, it was the biggest box office hit in Hollywood history. The combination of spectacular Alpine scenery, endearing children, sweeping Rodgers and Hammerstein melodies, and the fresh, joyous, beautiful face of Julie Andrews—plus a few villainous Nazis—proved irresistible to movie audiences around the world.

The film was carefully crafted by its primary creators: producer-director Robert Wise, his musical associate Saul Chaplin, screenwriter Ernest Lehman, musical director Irwin Kostal, and production designer Boris Leven. But Julie Andrews, in her third appearance before the cameras, provided the energy and spirit that keeps this confection aloft. No one involved in making the movie expected it to enjoy such stupendous success.

After weeks of expensive delays because of weather, the brilliant opening scene of The Sound of Music was finally filmed in a meadow near Mehlweg, Bavaria. It was the final location shot of the film.

Julie and director Robert Wise agreed that the film should strive to be less sugary than the stage musical. Wise insisted that the costumes and settings be understated, and Ernest Lehman added wit and genuine emotion to the script.

Julie takes a well-earned break on the set. Between guitar practice, music and dance rehearsals, costume

fittings, and instructions for operating the marionettes, she had a daunting daily schedule.

The real Maria Von Trapp (left) on the set of The Sound of Music *with Julie and Pat Wise, the director's late wife. Mrs. Von*

Trapp appeared as an extra in the film, crossing behind a row of columns during the song "I Have Confidence."

"My Favorite Things" was the first musical sequence to be filmed. Julie worked well with the seven children in the movie, and they adored their time with her. She told a reporter that the children were all "enchanting, very professional, disciplined, and sweet."

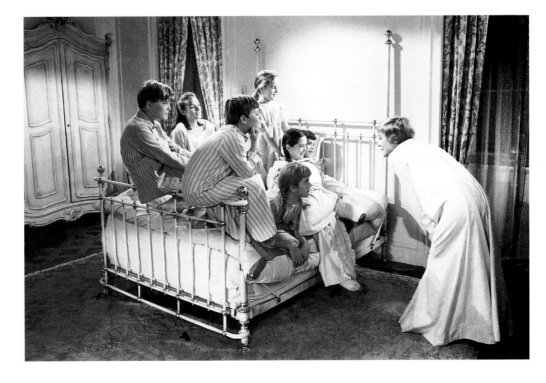

The flavor of old world Austria was captured by the film's choreographers in "The Laendler," a composite folk dance performed by the captain and the governess in this series of publicity photos.

Charismatic classical actor Christopher Plummer portrayed Captain Von Trapp, the stern widower who falls in love with his children's governess. The climactic declaration of love was musicalized with "Something Good," an exquisite new ballad writ-

ten especially for the film by Richard Rodgers. In press interviews conducted on the set, Christopher Plummer said that he "adored working with Julie and respected her talent immensely." She remarked that he was "marvelous to work with."

In the dramatic scenes between the young novitiate and the Mother Abbess (Peggy Wood), Julie's performance is notable for its restraint, conviction, and genuine feeling. It also earned her a second Oscar nomination.

A key ingredient in the success of the film is its breathtaking locations in the Austrian Alps. The "Do-Re-Mi" montage is a joyous travelogue for the city of Salzburg, which now offers visitors a "Sound of Music" tour.

The wedding gown by designer Dorothy Jeakins—indeed, the entire wedding sequence—is memorable for its special grace. However, the church was unheated and bitter cold. Julie remembers freezing in the paper-thin gown while trying to appear the radiant bride. In the background of this scene are Peggy Wood as the Mother Abbess (far left) and Anna Lee as Sister Margaretta. Wood was nominated for an Academy Award as Best Supporting Actress.

Julie posing with Richard Rodgers at the world premiere of The Sound of Music, *held at the Rivoli Theatre in New York on March 2, 1965. Following the screening, there was a special tribute to Oscar Hammerstein, who had died before the filming of his last musical work. The* *West Coast premiere was March 10, at the Fox Wilshire Theatre in Los Angeles. Julie was escorted by Christopher Plummer and her good friend Roddy McDowall. In a quaint bit of Hollywood whimsy, the children from* The Sound of Music *arrived together in a horse-drawn cart.*

The Sound of Music *broke all previous box office records. Devoted fans saw it dozens, even hundreds of times; and in many urban areas, the picture occupied the same first-run theater for more than a year. The phenomenal success of the film made Julie Andrews a superstar and one of the most famous and beloved women in the world.*

When Julie caught her
first glimpse of Makua
Beach in Hawaii, she
gasped: "What beautiful
scenery to chew!" Based
on the bestselling novel by
James Michener, *Hawaii is*
indeed the type of epic
period melodrama that
invites scenery chewing.
Julie's role as Jerusha
Bromley Hale, a New
England missionary's
wife, seemed an unex-
pected bit of casting for a
vivacious musical comedy
performer.

Still, Julie was such a
hot commodity—and such
a skillful actress—that she
made it all work. Despite
a lukewarm reaction from
the press, this very costly
picture made money, and
Julie provided a convinc-
ing performance. Her
youthful beauty is particularly striking in the earlier
New England settings.

Julie, as Jerusha Bromley, poses with her film family: (from left) Heather Menzies (Louisa in The Sound of Music), Elizabeth Cole, Carroll O'Connor (pre-"All in the Family"), and Diane Sherry. The richly detailed costumes of well-to-do Yankees in the 1820s were designed by Dorothy Jeakins.

Max Von Sydow (right) is the religious zealot who marries Jerusha and takes her to Hawaii. Richard Harris, the handsome sea captain she truly loves, later follows her to the islands. The New England scenes were filmed on location at Old Sturbridge Village in Massachusetts.

Director George Roy Hill discussing a scene with Julie. Hill was replaced briefly when the picture began to go over budget. Julie was among many in the cast who defended his work, and eventually Hill was able to finish the film.

Julie arrives for the world premiere of Hawaii *at the DeMille Theatre in New York, October 9, 1966. Bert Parks conducted interviews with the arriving celebrities, and Max Von Sydow joined Julie at the party. A West Coast premiere followed at Hollywood's Egyptian Theatre on October 13. Julie attended the second celebration with her new beau, director-writer Blake Edwards. "My Wishing Doll," sung by Julie in the movie, was nominated for an Oscar.*

Like many big-budget movies of the sixties, Hawaii *was distributed as a road-show presentation, playing in selected theaters with a reserved-seat policy and colorful souvenir programs sold in the lobby.*

'TORN CURTAIN'

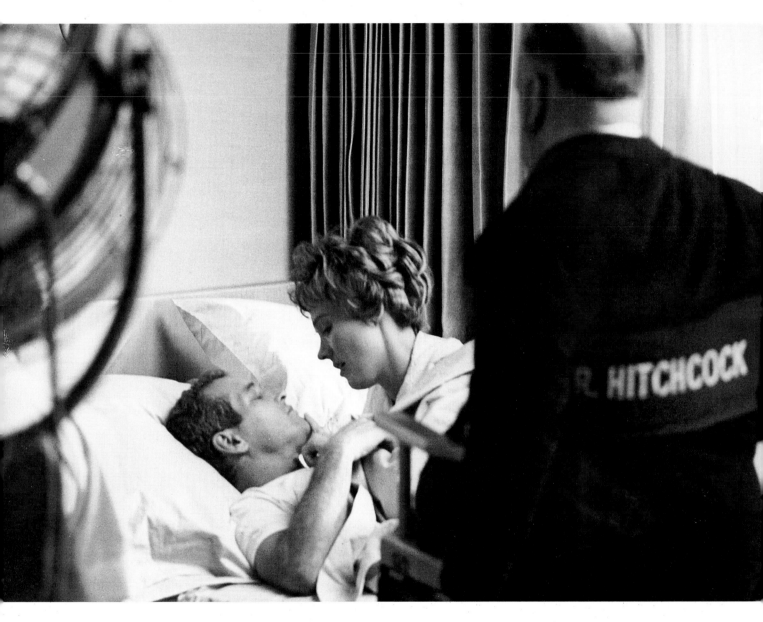

Director Alfred Hitchcock was at the peak of his popularity when he announced that his newest thriller would star Julie Andrews and Paul Newman, the hottest actors in Hollywood. The combination spelled box office magic; the film, released in July of 1966, was among the top ten pictures of that year. It is one of Hitchcock's lesser efforts, however, and Julie and Paul were given little to work with.

Set in East Germany, this tale of espionage places Sarah Sherman (Julie) in grave danger when she follows her fiancé, Nobel scientist Michael Armstrong (Newman), behind the iron curtain. For the two stars, the best moment occurs at the very outset of the movie when they are engaged in a playful and convincingly sexy love scene (above). Note the huge fan (left) that cools the "hot" proceedings.

Julie's pleasant relationship with Mr. Hitchcock began on the first day of shooting when she discovered that the practical-joking director had torn all the curtains in her dressing room. Hitchcock and his wife (below left) are joined by his stars in a celebration of Torn Curtain, *his fiftieth film. Because this was Julie's first film in a contemporary setting, several hairstyles were tried to give her a newer, sexier look. Here, in a costume test (below right), she poses in a white knit dress by legendary Hollywood designer Edith Head.*

About his costar Paul Newman once remarked, "She is the last of the really great broads." Julie adored his slangy American compliment. Hitchcock was also complimentary, despite his reputation for disliking most actors. At a press conference, he took special note of Julie's beauty and added, "She is one of those people whose strength and talent comes across on the screen."

The plot of Torn Curtain can be boiled down to an extended chase of the hero and heroine by various East German villains. Here, in a scene from the chase, Julie and Paul are aided by an eccentric German countess, portrayed by the charming European actress Lila Kedrova (Zorba the Greek).

Small-town girl Millie Dilmount comes to New York City at the height of the Roaring Twenties to find secretarial work and marry her boss. In the hilarious opening sequence of the film, Millie realizes that if she is to achieve her goal, she'll have to become a "Modern." In a series of memorable comic bits, Millie alters her appearance from "good goody girl" to flaming flapper.

Producer Ross Hunter had loved Julie's performance on Broadway in The Boy Friend *and tried to get the film rights from* MGM. *When he was unsuccessful, he opted to create* an original twenties vehicle for Julie. In the course of development, the movie grew from a little comedy with incidental music to a full-scale musical and the highest grossing film in Universal's fifty-two-year history.

Julie Andrews's box office appeal was the key to the film's success, of course, but it is also blessed with a delightful cast, an effervescent score of familiar songs, and Ross Hunter's typical attention to stylish and colorful production design.

"THOROUGHLY MODERN MILLIE"

Millie and Jimmy (James Fox) dance a variation of the Charleston called "The Tapioca." Ross Hunter and director George Roy Hill elected to use one pre- dominant color in each major scene (yellow, in this case) in order to give the movie the look of a hand-tinted black-and- white silent film.

At a special launch party at Chasen's restaurant in Beverly Hills, Julie and Mary Tyler Moore joined the guest of honor, Beatrice Lillie. The irresistible cast, posed here for a publicity photo (below), includes Beatrice Lillie as Mrs. Meers, the bumbling "white-slaver"; James Fox as a young millionaire-in-disguise; Carol Channing as zany heiress Muzzy Van Hossmere; John Gavin as the "eligible boss"; and Mary Tyler Moore in a wonderful performance as innocent Miss Dorothy.

Millie (above left) just moments before she becomes an "unspeakably fatal" vamp (below right). Her handsome employer (Gavin, below left) falls instead for the old-fashioned charms of Mary Tyler Moore. The boarding-house elevator (above right) operates only if its passengers are tap dancing. Joe Layton's witty choreography for Julie and Mary is a high-light of the film.

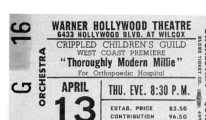

The world premiere of Thoroughly Modern Millie *was held at New York's Criterion Theatre on March 21, 1967. The West Coast premiere (pictured), at the Warner Hollywood Theatre on April 13, featured usherettes dressed as flappers. Special guests, including Lucille Ball, Maureen O'Hara, Rosalind Russell, and Carol Burnett, arrived at the theater in vintage automobiles. Producer Ross Hunter is seen below at the premiere, happily embracing his leading lady.*

STAR!

While Julie was starring in My Fair Lady, *parallels were drawn between her career and that of English stage legend Gertrude Lawrence. The possibility of a stage show or movie musical about Miss Lawrence, with Julie in the lead, was mentioned even then. However, other than the fact that both women began as young-sters in British music hall and went on to become great ladies of the theater, they couldn't have been less similar. Gertrude Lawrence was thought of as difficult, neurotic, extravagant, and self-consumed. Julie shares none of these qualities.*

Thus, despite Julie's compelling performance in STAR!, the much antic-ipated film biography of Gertrude Lawrence, the audience was uncomfort-able with her unsympa-thetic character. They were further distanced by the decision of the movie's creators, producer Saul Chaplin and director Robert Wise, to use a doc-umentary approach to Lawrence's story.

The picture opened with much fanfare as a road-show attraction. It even included an overture before each showing. But the box office receipts were disappointing, even after the studio cut an

hour out of the movie and released it with a cheery new title, Those Were the Happy Times.

Despite its problems, STAR! *includes fifteen musical numbers and some of Julie's finest moments on film. She*

appears in almost every scene of the three-hour movie, looking dazzling in an array of chic outfits by designer Donald Brooks. She sings timeless songs by Gershwin, Coward, Porter, and Weill. And the production numbers, bril-

liantly staged by Michael Kidd, reveal the incredible range of Julie's talents. STAR! *may not have been a box office sensation, but it presented a sensational Julie Andrews!*

Saul Chaplin and Robert Wise browse with Julie at Cartier's, one of Gertie Lawrence's haunts. The producers began developing STAR! *while working with Julie on* The Sound of Music.

In a costume test for the film, Julie models a button-covered "Pearlie" outfit designed for a music hall segment. Donald Brooks created a record 125 costumes for Julie's portrayal of Gertrude Lawrence, a notorious clothes horse.

A typically busy moment on the set, with the star attended by two wardrobe women, a makeup artist, a property assistant, and choreographer Michael Kidd, who is checking Julie's footwear.

"The Saga of Jenny," from the Kurt Weill, Ira Gershwin, Moss Hart musical Lady in the Dark, was the most demanding production number in the film. According to Michael Kidd, Julie executed most of the difficult circus stunts without a stand-in. Julie recalls, "I did everything from knockabout comedy to sophisticated dance, from acrobatic stuff to bumps and grinds."

This scene, a Depression-era dance marathon, appears in a montage depicting Gertie's efforts to pay off debt accumulated through her profligate lifestyle.

STAR-1254

STAR-1255

STAR-1256

STAR-671

STAR-672

STAR-673

STAR-1246

STAR-1247

STAR-1248

"Burlington Bertie from Bow" (center) is one of Julie's favorite numbers from STAR! The other film strips are glamour shots taken for publicity.

Richard Crenna (above right) played Gertrude Lawrence's husband, Richard Aldrich, apparently the only man able to handle the difficult star. Aldrich himself was a visitor to the set of STAR!, where he noted, "It's remarkable how much Miss Andrews reminds me of Gertrude." Robert Reed (top left), who was to become famous for "The Brady Bunch," played another of Lawrence's American suitors. Reed recalled that he would come to the set on his days off to watch Julie rehearse, and that he was awestruck by her discipline. The casting of Daniel Massey (left) as Lawrence's lifelong friend and collaborator Noel Coward was suggested by Mr. Coward himself.

The press had begun to snipe at Julie and made much of the fact that she missed the world premiere of STAR! *in London and the New York opening as well, because she was in Ireland with Blake Edwards filming* Darling Lili. *She and Blake did attend the West Coast premiere of the film, October 31, 1968, at the Fox Wilshire Theatre in Los Angeles. ABC taped the event for "The Joey Bishop Show," with Regis Philbin interviewing the arriving guests. STAR! was* heavily promoted, and it performed respectably for a time. But ultimately the returns were disappointing, and Hollywood word of mouth termed the film a box office failure. At right, a shop window in London features an animated lobby display for the film, with photographs, soundtrack album, and sheet music.

In an ad (above right) for the reissued, renamed movie, note the conscious effort of the ad designers to evoke the look and spirit of The Sound of Music.

DARLING LILI

Darling Lili, *the first collaboration between Julie and Blake Edwards, is an entertaining, well-crafted, often-funny, always-beautiful movie musical. Unfortunately, it suffered mortally from its outsized budget and the public relations fallout over* STAR! *The press was now gunning for Julie and Blake, Hollywood's golden couple, and it dismissed* Darling Lili *as a total fiasco brought on by the hubris of its director-writer and star.*

The times were a-changing as well—the movie was released in 1970, when audiences had lost interest in conventional, big-budget American movies—and most especially in escapist movie musicals.

Julie has several great moments in the film, including its haunting opening scene set to "Whistling Away the Dark," a pretty ballad by Henry Mancini and Johnny Mercer. Blake Edwards created a lavish and affectionate valentine for his new lady love; he also tried to reveal the witty, worldly woman who had become lost in the avalanche of publicity

for Mary Poppins *and* The Sound of Music.

Shooting began on March 18, 1968, and Darling Lili *finally premiered, after much tinkering by the studio, on June 23, 1970. The reviews and the initial run at Radio City Music Hall were encouraging, but the picture had little box office impact in the rest of the country and quickly disappeared from theaters.*

Filmed in the lovely old Gaiety Theater in Dublin, the scene at right depicts Lili calming her audience during an air raid. With such World War I standards as "Keep the Home Fires Burning" and "It's a Long Way to Tipperary," the scene was reminiscent of Julie's own childhood experiences in the bomb shelters of London, where her stepfather Ted Andrews sang for their frightened and exhausted neighbors.

According to Blake and Julie, some of the romantic dialogue for Julie and her costar Rock Hudson is based on the Andrews-Edwards real-life courtship. At right, the two take a break on location at the ornate Palace of Justice in Brussels.

Julie portrays Lili Smith, a popular English entertainer during World War I. She is, in fact, Lili Schmit, a spy for the imperial German forces. Lili's prime target is an American fly-boy, Major William Larrabee (Rock Hudson), whom she seduces in an effort to extract military secrets. Instead, Lili falls in love with him, and the movie unravels this not-so-comic predicament.

When Lili discovers that Major Larrabee is intrigued by a beautiful stripper, she turns her prim music hall solo into a striptease. It's a wonderfully performed and edited comedy sequence, and it provides the first glimpse of Blake and Julie's determination to break away from her Mary Poppins–Sound of Music image. The ads for Darling Lili proclaimed that "she sizzles, she dances, she spies."

The film premiered in Hollywood at the Cinerama Dome, with Julie and Blake joined by Rock Hudson and his guest Flo Allen. Despite (or perhaps because of) ads encouraging families to return to "good clean entertainment," the film never recovered its huge investment. It is the only Julie Andrews film that has never been released on home video.

Julie personally requested the services of her STAR! costumer Donald Brooks, who created a stunning wardrobe for her portrayal of Lili. The World War I fashions are particularly suited to Julie, who is radiant in every frame of this movie.

Blake Edwards (left), whose real forte is comedy, directed and wrote this thriller, released in the summer of 1974. The movie made money, particularly overseas, but it was not perceived as a success at home. In addition to the cozy romantic scenes between Julie and costar Omar Sharif, the chief merits of the film are its beautiful location scenery in Switzerland and Barbados, the warm appeal of Sharif, and the opportunity to see Julie looking svelte and sexy in a bikini.

The Tamarind Seed, based on a spy novel by Evelyn Anthony, was the second Andrews-Edwards effort. Julie plays Judith Farrow, a young widow working at the British Foreign Office; Omar Sharif is Feodor Sverdlov, an agent of the Soviet secret service. While on vacation in Barbados, Judith falls for the charming, handsome Feodor, and their passionate affair plunges them into a nightmare of international espionage.

The Tamarind Seed

About Omar Sharif Julie said, "He's a most considerate actor, and I've always adored that aura of quiet romance that he exudes. I found he cares very much about your feelings." And about his feelings, Sharif once said, "Where else but in the movies could I make love to a woman like Julie Andrews and get paid for it?"

In his first major role in an American film, Dudley Moore was launched into genuine movie stardom by "10." Julie, on the other hand, was more or less overlooked in the role of Samantha, Moore's faithful and underappreciated girlfriend.

"10" was Julie's third film with Blake and, by coincidence, her tenth motion picture. The photograph opposite is a candid of the husband-wife team on location in Beverly Hills.

The striking portraits of Julie with Dudley Moore and Bo Derek were created on location on a Mexican beach.

"10"

After a break of nearly six years, in which Julie devoted time to her family, to television, and to a concert tour, she returned to movies with a small role in Blake Edwards's super-hit comedy, "10."

Released October 5, 1979, the film was an enormous success, both financially and artistically, and put Blake back on the Hollywood map.

The movie's title refers to the male practice of rating women from 1 to 10, and the "10" in this case was Bo Derek (opposite). Bo became an overnight celebrity—the world's media went wild over this exquisitely beautiful young woman.

"10" is not a musical, but Julie can be heard singing on Moore's car radio, and she and Dudley perform a very touching duet, "It's Easy to Say," composed by Henry Mancini. Julie's new hairstyle reflects her first contemporary role as a liberated woman, comfortable with the graphic language and subject matter of Blake's film. It was the first Julie Andrews movie to get an R rating.

LITTLE MISS MARKER

This was the fourth film adaptation of the classic story by Damon Runyon. (Shirley Temple's 1934 version was the first.) In this rendering, also set in the Depression era, Julie plays Amanda, a down-on-her-luck socialite who fronts a gambling operation to regain her estate. She becomes involved with a bookie, Sorrowful Jones (Walter Matthau), who accepts a little girl (Sara Stimson) as a marker for her father's gambling debts.

Julie was eager to work with Matthau, and she found the screenplay "really charming." But it was screenwriter Walter Bernstein's first directing job; and despite Matthau, Andrews, and a sweet performance by Sara Stimson, the critics dismissed it as inconsequential. Its release, March 21, 1980, was given little promotion, and the movie disappeared quickly from the nation's theaters.

After much persuasion, squeaky-clean screen darling Sally Miles agrees to bare her "boobies" to assure the financial success of a movie by her unhinged ex-husband. Here, tanked on champagne and tranquilizers, Sally is escorted from her trailer by the director (William Holden). She is tottering on the set and awaiting the cue to open her robe (below). Julie's "nude scene" was one of the most talked-about events of her career. Playboy magazine even featured frames of an undraped Julie in their year-end "sex in cinema" issue.

S.O.B. *stands for "Standard Operating Bull." It was writer-director Blake Edwards's satirical revenge on Hollywood for the pressures and ugly behaviors he encountered during the making of* Darling Lili. *Ironically, Paramount Studios, the source of much of Blake's grief on* Lili, *also released* S.O.B., *although by that time studio head Robert Evans (the Robert Vaughn character?) had been replaced.*

The wacky story concerns a movie producer (Richard Mulligan) who has a nervous breakdown when his most recent picture becomes a colossal bomb. The studio cuts off funding for a musical he is currently creating for his wife, a film star with a wholesome public image very much like Julie's. He decides that he will regain his film project and save his career by turning the new project into a soft-porn film allegory in which his wife will expose her breasts and thereby attract millions to the box office.

S.O.B. *didn't quite attract those millions. The film opened in major cities on July 1, 1981, and it received decent notices but only modest box office returns. The script was probably too sophisticated and "inside Hollywood" for a mass audience. Nonetheless,* S.O.B. *is a lot of fun; and Julie's willingness to take on this relatively small role, disrobe, and then endure the inevitable press frenzy, is* proof positive that she and Blake have a loving, highly supportive relationship, as well as a healthy sense of humor.

The stellar (and hilarious) cast of S.O.B.: *(from left) Loretta Swit, Robert Loggia, Craig Stevens, Larry Hagman, William Holden, Julie, Richard Mulligan, Robert Preston, Robert Vaughn, Larry Storch, Benson Fong, Shelley Winters, Stuart Margolin, Marisa Berenson, and Robert Webber.*

With *Victor/Victoria,
Blake Edwards created the
perfect vehicle for his own
and his wife's wide-
ranging talents. Based on
a 1933 German film
Viktor und Viktoria, the
farcical plot involves
Victoria Grant, a down-at-
heels English soprano who
pretends to be a gay Polish
count, Victor Grazinski, in
order to land a job in a
Parisian drag club. In
short, Julie plays a woman
pretending to be a man
impersonating a woman.*

Blake had enjoyed his
greatest career successes
with physical comedy—
most notably, the Pink
Panther series—and the
story of Victor/Victoria
provided countless oppor-
tunities for all the mishaps
and mistaken identities of
good farce.

Julie also has a great
gift for comedy, but audiences had never before
seen her talent for mim-
icry, nor had they heard
the rich lower ranges of
her voice. She was uneasy
about the role and
worked hard to acquire
the characteristic move-
ments and gestures of a
male. When her prepara-
tions were done, she cre-

ated a very plausible (and
funny) Victor for the cameras.

The film was produced
at England's Pinewood
Studios, where all nine
soundstages were used to
create the elegantly styl-
ized Parisian sets by
Rodgers Maus. Robert
Preston played Toddy, a
gay boulevardier who
befriends Victoria and
comes up with the scheme
to invent Victor. James

Garner portrays King
Marchan, the Chicago
gangster who sees Victor
at the club and is
unnerved to find himself
attracted to him. Lesley
Ann Warren is priceless as
Garner's high-strung, low-
wattage girlfriend,
Norma; and Alex Karras
is especially endearing as
Squash, Garner's sensitive
bodyguard.

With its beautiful sets,
splendid score (by Henry

Mancini and Leslie
Bricusse), uproarious
comedy, and superb cast,
Victor/Victoria *was a solid
hit at the box office. Julie,
Robert Preston, and
Lesley Ann Warren were
all nominated for Oscars,
as were Mancini's score
and Maus's production
design. In 1995, Blake
and Julie revamped
Victor/Victoria *as a stage
musical and took it to
Broadway.

Victor/Victoria is the masterpiece (at least to date) of the Andrews-Edwards partnership. This photograph (above left), taken on the set at Pinewood Studios, seems to indicate some happiness with their situation. Robert Preston (above right) was a close friend of Julie and Blake's and the perfect actor to defuse for audiences the potentially troubling topic of homosexuality. The famous cockroach-in-my-salad scene (bottom) has already entered the movie history books as an exemplary bit of great comic filmmaking.

Julie taught herself to walk, talk, and fight like a man. Here, as Victor, she both wallops and nuzzles King, played by her old friend and costar James Garner. Victor (at right) becomes "The Shady Dame from Seville" in a delightful drag flamenco, which is also performed later by Robert Preston.

Victor/Victoria *premiered
on March 16, 1982, at the
Plitt Century Plaza
Theatre in Los Angeles.
Lesley Ann Warren joined
other members of the cast
for the opening night fes-
tivities. Julie's parents,
Sean Connery, Barry
Manilow, Ginger Rogers,
and Cary Grant were
among the guests at the
party, which was set up
like a European street fair,
with food carts and traveling musicians.*

The Man Who Loved Women

Blake Edwards adapted François Truffaut's 1977 French comedy for his tale of a womanizing sculptor, David Fowler (Burt Reynolds), who visits a psychiatrist, Marianna (Julie), in an effort to relieve his creative block.

Instead, the two fall in love and then deal with the comic complications of their situation.

Blake wrote this bittersweet comedy in collaboration with his own analyst, Milton Wexler. Julie worked closely with her therapist to develop a plausible couchside manner.

The film was not very well received when it opened (December 16, 1983). Most critics felt it was not up to Blake's usual standards. Julie does everything she can to keep the romantic comedy moving along. As for Burt, she had this to say: "Working with him is a joy. He is such a consummate artist, and he does it so well. He makes it easy for us ladies."

120

THAT'S LIFE!

That's Life *was truly a family affair, with Blake and Julie's daughters Jennifer Edwards (left) and Emma Walton (right) and Jack Lemmon's son Chris (center) playing principal roles in the film. Felicia Farr, Lemmon's real-life wife (and Chris's mother), also appeared as a fortune-teller in the film. The story grew out of Blake's highly personal thirteen-page treatment about a man in midlife crisis. Much of the dialogue was improvised by the actors, and the movie was shot at Blake and Julie's Malibu home. They would literally wake up and go to work in their own bedroom.*

As Gillian Fairchild, Julie plays the steady, long-suffering wife of a self-absorbed, philandering hypochondriac named Harry (Jack Lemmon). While Gillian is waiting anxiously for the results of a biopsy on her throat, her oblivious family bickers and frets about their personal problems while preparing for Harry's sixtieth birthday.

This rather serious and poignant Edwards's film is interesting not only for its insights into the male ego, but also for its surprisingly intimate glimpse of the Andrews-Edwards family itself. Blake maintained an extremely low budget for this "family movie," and it was a mod-erate success upon its release September 26, 1986.

At the time Julie said, "It's sort of a dream come true. It's Emma's first major role in a film. She has been working very seriously toward her acting career, and for us to do her first film together is like being handed a wonderful gift." Julie and Emma have two terrific scenes together in the film, and Julie pulls out all the stops in the climax of the film with an angry rebuke of her husband, which must have resonated very deeply in Julie and Blake's own lives.

At the New York premiere for the film, Julie was quoted as saying, "I don't know that I'm quite as patient as the lady I play on the screen. I think I blow off steam a lot more than she does." Blake demurred: "Not true, not true!"

Duet *for* ONE

Julie returned to England for the production of Duet for One, *which was based on a two-character play by Tom Kempinski. With the help of a brilliant cast and a sensitive Russian filmmaker, Andrei Konchalovsky, Julie created the finest dramatic work of her career. She plays Stephanie Anderson,* a virtuoso concert violinist struck down by multiple sclerosis. Old friend Max Von Sydow portrays her psychiatrist, and Alan Bates plays her estranged husband.

Julie studied for weeks to give the appearance of playing the violin, and she spent time meeting people with multiple sclerosis at a clinic in Bromley, Kent. She called her role "the most desperate and emotionally pained woman I've ever played." Julie captured the character's bitterness and anguish in several brutal scenes which earned critical acclaim for both the film and her performance. The dramatic climax, a lengthy silent scene between Julie and the movie camera, is a shocker.

Duet for One *opened in December 1986 and played mainly limited runs in art houses around the country. Neither the film nor Julie received the attention they deserved.*

The stricken violinist (at right) with Max Von Sydow (left), Alan Bates, and actress Cathryn Harrison, Rex Harrison's granddaughter. Rupert Everett (below right) portrays Stephanie's star pupil. Director Andrei Konchalovsky stands between them in the scene, which was filmed in London's famous Royal Albert Hall. An itinerant young scrap merchant (Liam Neeson, below) is enticed into a brief affair with the lonely woman.

A Fine Romance

Julie's most recent movie was based on Tchin-Tchin, a popular play. The title refers to an intimate toast spoken with the clink of wine glasses. Julie plays an Englishwoman, Pamela Picquet, who agrees to meet Cesareo Gramaldi (Marcello Mastroianni) to discuss the affair currently underway between her husband and his wife. In an attempt to resolve their mutual problem, they fall into their own affair, which is carried out in some very attractive Parisian settings.

Broadway director Gene Saks created this somewhat talky adult comedy, which opened September 11, 1992, and had a very limited run. Julie and Marcello worked well together, and they certainly enjoyed the experience. About Mastroianni Julie said, "His timing, his sense of comedy, his knowledge of himself and of life is wonderful to see. He's the easiest, most natural man to work with. He's a darling human being, very gentle and kind." A Fine Romance was released in Europe as Tchin-Tchin or Cin-Cin. In Japan it was known as Afternoon Tea in Bed.

1. *London production of* My Fair Lady; *photograph by Cecil Beaton*

2 & 3. The Boy Friend

4. *"High Tor"*

5 & 6. My Fair Lady

7 & 8. Cinderella

9. *Authorized Julie Andrews paper dolls, circa 1958*

10. *British ladies' magazine, 1958*

11, 12, & 13. Camelot

14 & 15. *"Julie and Carol at Carnegie Hall"*

16. *First husband Tony Walton and daughter Emma Kate, 1963*

17. *"The Andy Williams Show"*

18 & 19. Mary Poppins

20. The Americanization of Emily

21. *"The Julie Andrews Show"*

22 & 23. The Sound of Music

2

4

3

5

6

7

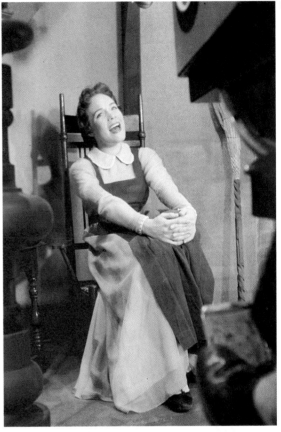

8

9

10

11

12

13

14

15

16

17

18

19

20

24

25

26

27

29

28

33

34

35

36

38

37

39

40

41

46

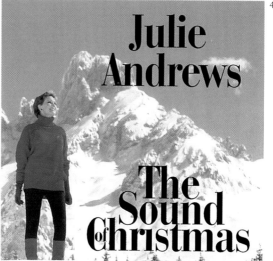

47

48

49

50

52

51

53

24 & 25. The Sound of Music

26. The handprint ceremony, Grauman's Chinese Theatre, 1966

27 & 28. Thoroughly Modern Millie

29 & 30. STAR!

31 & 32. Darling Lili

33. "An Evening with Julie Andrews and Harry Belafonte"

34, 35, & 36. "The Julie Andrews Hour," with guest stars Robert Goulet, James Stewart, and Cass Elliot

37. Theme song for "The Julie Andrews Hour"; music by Julie Andrews, lyrics by Leslie Bricusse

38. Portrait, 1972

39. Blake and Julie's adopted children, Amy and Joanna

40. "10"

41. Las Vegas act, 1976

42 & 43. Victor/Victoria

44. Golden Globe Award for Victor/Victoria, *1983*

45. Publicity shot for That's Life, *with daughter Emma Walton*

46. With director Andrei Konchalovsky on the set of Duet for One

47. Record sleeve for The Sound of Christmas

48. "Julie and Carol Together Again"

49. The newly named Julie Andrews Rose at the 1992 Chelsea Flower Show in London

50. Julie with Blake, 1991

51. Putting It Together

52 & 53. Broadway's Victor/Victoria

4
Television

People tend to take television for granted as a kind of disposable entertainment medium with minimal artistic content. Julie never seemed to see it that way. Unlike many major stars, she has welcomed opportunities to make television appearances throughout her career. And unlike many people in the television business, she has taken the medium seriously, devoting as much time and thought and effort to her television work as she does to her movie roles or recordings or concerts.

As a consequence, Julie is responsible for dozens of memorable television performances. Her very first special, with guest star Gene Kelly, received glowing notices, including this comment from the critic for *Daily Variety*: "There should have been a national proclamation of Julie Andrews Night. She is the best thing that has happened to television, and gives the medium new stature and dimension far beyond the abused word of 'special.'"

Perhaps the greatest merit of her TV variety appearances is that they show us the *real* Julie Andrews—the singer, the music hall trouper, the consummate entertainer unrestricted by the requirements of a dramatic role which may or may not be a perfect fit. She has also created some wonderful television *roles*, of course, but the more direct encounters between Julie Andrews and the TV cameras are the moments that tend to live on in our memories. Julie's extraordinary gifts as an entertainer are inseparable from her genuinely warm and generous personality.

Julie made her first television appearances as a child on the BBC in the earliest days of the medium. Once she had conquered Broadway,

she became a frequent guest star on American television variety shows. She generally preferred to perform new musical material rather than songs from her current stage repertoire, and, as a result, the television archives are rich with Julie's performances of everything from English folk ballads to Top 40 hits.

Even during her busiest Hollywood years in the sixties, Julie made a number of television appearances; in the 1970s she hosted her own award-winning variety series as well as a string of specials. Most of her important television appearances are represented in this chapter.

"High Tor" (CBS, March 10, 1956). The Guinness Book of Records *lists this musical drama as the first made-for-television movie. Based on a verse play by Maxwell Anderson, "High Tor" was filmed in Hollywood in November 1955. Bing Crosby, who had seen Julie in* The Boy Friend, *requested her as his leading lady, and she made her first trip to Hollywood for this project. She played Lise, a phantom Dutch girl on High Tor mountain. The musical was presented as part of the "Ford Star Jubilee" series. It had been announced as a pioneer CBS color production, but ultimately was telecast in black and white.*

"The Ed Sullivan Show" (CBS, July 15 and November 11, 1956). Julie made her first two appearances on this weekly live broadcast in order to publicize My Fair Lady. She sang "I Could Have Danced All Night" and "Show Me" in the July appearance. (Sullivan introduced "Show Me" as "Words, Words, Words.") Julie's second appearance was part of a special tribute to Life magazine. Her medley for the program consisted of "Wouldn't It Be Loverly?," "I'll Follow My Secret Heart," and "Someone to Watch over Me."

"Cinderella" (CBS, March 31, 1957). One of the most famous broadcasts in the history of television, Rodgers and Hammerstein's "Cinderella" was seen by an audience of 107 million people. Oscar Hammerstein II (left) and Richard Rodgers (right) wrote the musical especially for Julie and for television. The telecast was seen live and in color in the eastern time zones and as a black-and-white kinescope (created during a dress rehearsal) in the rest of the country. Julie received her first Emmy nomination for this memorable program.

This romantic ball gown, perfect for a princess-to-be, was used solely for publicity photographs.

The actual gown for the telecast is simpler and more elegant. It was also easier for Julie to manage in the narrow confines of the live television settings.

With "A Lovely Night," Cinderella's hilariously nasty stepsisters, Alice Ghostley (opposite left) and Kaye Ballard (center), recount their experiences at the ball. Julie's step-mother was played by Ilka Chase, a distinguished Broadway comedian. The Fairy Godmother, played by Edie Adams (above), sings the sprightly "Impossible, It's Possible" as she escorts Cinderella to the ball. At the ball, the prince (Jon Cypher) meets Cinderella in the palace garden and sings a beautiful Rodgers and Hammerstein ballad, "Do I Love You Because You're Beautiful."

"The Dinah Shore Show" (NBC, January 12, 1958). As a guest star on this weekly color series, Julie sang "Blue Moon" and joined Dinah and Chita Rivera in a rousing "Life upon the Wicked Stage" from Showboat. Julie holds music for the song "Whispering Hope."

"The Big Record" (CBS, February 5, 1958). Recording star Patti Page hosted this weekly music program telecast live from New York. This episode featured a variety of musical styles with Roberta Sherwood, Woody Herman and his Orchestra, the Everly Brothers, and a duet by Julie and Patti.

"*The Jack Benny Hour*" (CBS, May 23, 1959). During Julie and Tony Walton's honeymoon in California, she appeared on this Jack Benny special singing a medley from My Fair Lady and "Summertime" from Porgy and Bess. *The finale of the show was a skit called "The Defiant Ones Like It Hot," which spoofed two popular movies of the time. The* skit featured Julie, dressed as a flapper, singing "I'm Just Wild About Harry," "Ain't We Got Fun," and "Music, Music, Music." Jack Benny offered blessings for her new marriage, and Phil Silvers asked to dance with the bride. The show was rerun in 1963 as "The Comedy Hour Special." Jack Benny greets Julie and her new husband at Los Angeles Airport (below).

"The Julie Andrews Show" (BBC, November 12 to December 24, 1959).

In England, Julie hosted four programs of music and interviews, mainly with performers from her past. Guests included her parents and Vic Oliver from Starlight Roof. *Tony Walton was set designer for the series. The final episode (right) was telecast on Christmas Eve. Titled "The Gentle Flame," it was a musical version of Hans Christian Andersen's* The Little Match Girl, *featuring Julie as Trissa, the impoverished match girl who dreams of a better life.*

*"The Fabulous Fifties"
(CBS, January 31, 1960).
Covering the most popu-
lar books, films, plays,
and music of the previous
decade, this two-hour
prime-time special
included a fascinating segment in which Julie and
Rex Harrison (opposite)
recreated the rehearsal
process for* My Fair Lady.
*Julie was also shown
working with vocal coach
Alfred Dixon to perfect
her cockney accent. The
scene segued into her performance of "Just You
Wait" (right). This special
received an Emmy for
Outstanding Variety
Program. During the fol-
lowing week, Julie was
mystery guest on the game
show "What's My Line?"*

"The Bell Telephone Hour" (NBC, February 12, 1960).
This live "colorcast," titled "Portraits in Music," was hosted by Carl Sandburg. In a medley of operetta miniatures by Sigmund Romberg, Julie sang several selections, including "Lover, Come Back to Me" and "The Fireman's Bride" (pictured).

"The Ed Sullivan Show" (CBS, March 19, 1961). *This special tribute to Lerner and Loewe opened with Julie and Robert Goulet singing "Almost Like Being In Love" from* Brigadoon. *To celebrate the fifth anniversary of* My Fair Lady, *Julie slipped back into her Eliza costume to sing "Wouldn't It Be Loverly?" with a company of cockney singers. She also donned her Embassy Ball gown for "I Could Have Danced All Night." In the finale of the show, Julie joined Richard Burton to perform two songs, "Camelot" and "What Do the Simple Folk Do?," from their new Broadway show.*

"The Garry Moore Show" (CBS, May 2, September 26, and December 19, 1961, and May 1, 1962). Julie and Carol Burnett first became a team (and lifelong friends) during this weekly variety series, on which Julie made four guest appearances. In a regular segment called "That Wonderful Year" (in this case 1956), Julie and Carol wore outlandish cowboy hats for a production number of "Big D" from Most Happy Fella. The number was so well received that it was restaged for Julie and Carol's first special at Carnegie Hall. In the September 26 episode, Julie sang "Looking for a Boy" from her third solo album and "This Can't Be Love" from "Wonderful Year" 1939. Julie and Carol also joined in a tribute to The Wizard of Oz, singing "If I Only Had a Brain." MGM wouldn't permit them to wear the intended scarecrow costumes, so they performed in rehearsal clothes.

The December 19 outing was a Christmas show with Broadway favorite Gwen Verdon. For Julie's final guest appearance, the company saluted 1947 with a medley from Finian's Rainbow.

"The Broadway of Lerner and Loewe" (NBC, February 11, 1962). This exceptionally beautiful color telecast is one of television's finest hours. Julie sang "Show Me" and "With a Little Bit of Luck" and appeared in the regal throne-room scene from Camelot. *In the finale, Julie sang "I Could Have Danced All Night" with Maurice Chevalier, Robert Goulet, Richard Burton, and Stanley Holloway.*

*"Julie and Carol at
Carnegie Hall"*
*(CBS, June 11, 1962).
This acclaimed television
event, taped "live" in
New York on March 5,
received both an Emmy
for Outstanding Music
Program and a prestigious
Montreaux Festival
Award. A musical high-
light of the evening was
Julie and Carol's lyrical
and witty ten-minute med-
ley saluting the history of
musical comedy.*

"Julie and Carol at Carnegie Hall" was written by Mike Nichols and Ken Welch, who developed hilarious spoofs of "The Ed Sullivan Show" ("The Nausiev Dancers") and The Sound of Music *("The Pratt Family Singers"). Regarding the "Big D" number, pictured here in rehearsal and at the taping, Julie told the press, "I've always wanted to be a real cowgirl. I think I'd like to be wacky from now on." A concert tour of this very successful television special was under discussion until Julie discovered that she was pregnant.*

"*The Andy Williams Show*" (NBC, November 30, 1964).
This episode of the Williams series was taped in October when Julie had a little time between films. She promoted The Americanization of Emily *by running clips from the film while Andy counted her kisses with James Garner. She also sang* "Where Is Love" *with Andy and danced up a storm in an opening number called* "Fireworks" (left). *Andy's regulars, the Osmond Brothers* (below), *joined Julie in sweet renditions of* "Supercalifragilisticexpealidocious" *and* "Sing a Rainbow." *This special guest appearance won Julie another Emmy nomination.*

"The Julie Andrews Show" (NBC, November 28, 1965).

Julie's first television special is a work of art. This classy hour of music, dance, and comedy featured its star in top form, singing, dancing, and clowning with the New Christy Minstrels and special guest star Gene Kelly. Highlights of the special included a "family tree" segment (opposite) in which Julie recalled some "relatives": a bawdy music hall girl ("It's Men Like You"), a knight (singing "Camelot" through his helmet), and a Wagnerian soprano. Julie and Gene were a perfect team, and their ballroom rendition of "Just in Time" (opposite) was exquisite. Director Alan Handly won an Emmy for this special, which was shown three times on the network.

"An Evening with Julie Andrews and Harry Belafonte" (NBC, November 9, 1969). Julie's second special, directed by Broadway's Gower Champion (left), was at the same superb level as her first. Harry Belafonte was Julie's guest, and the program focused on the special talents of its two performers. With Belafonte at her side, Julie sang a relaxed and engaging version of the old folk song "I Know Where I'm Going," and the two sang and danced to a medley of contemporary songs, including "Scarborough Fair," "Feelin' Groovy," and "Abergavenny." The spectacular "Ring Bell" (opposite) featured a studio hung with dozens of bells.

"The Grand Opening of Walt Disney World" (NBC, October 29, 1971). Julie danced around the sparkling new theme park singing Disney's "Zip-a-Dee-Doo-Dah" and "When You Wish upon a Star." In Fantasyland, Julie joined children dressed in costumes from many countries to sing "Wonderful World Full of Love."

"Julie and Carol at Lincoln Center" (CBS, December 7, 1971). Julie and Carol's second special was taped live on July 1 at the new Philharmonic Hall (now Avery Fisher Hall) in Lincoln Center. Julie sang a moody ballad, "He's Gone Away," and the pair harmonized in a charming medley celebrating songs of the sixties. The joyous finale, "Wait Till the Sun Shines, Nellie," featured Julie and Carol singing and dancing in galoshes and bright yellow slickers.

"The Julie Andrews Hour" (ABC, 24 episodes, September 13, 1972, to March 31, 1973). In this lavish series of variety shows, Julie was teamed with a surprising range of guest stars, including Angela Lansbury, Robert Goulet, Cass Elliot, Joel Grey, Peggy Lee, and the Smothers Brothers. Special episodes saluted the English music hall and the forties (left, in a wartime musical spoof with guest star Steve Lawrence and series regulars Rich Little and Alice Ghostley). Sammy Davis, Jr. (bottom left), persuaded Julie to try rock and roll, and Sid Caesar engaged her in a comedy sketch that was cut from the show.

The first episode of "The Julie Andrews Hour" showcased her career and included a medley from The Boy Friend *and a* rousing Charleston with her dancers (right). The shows were initially taped before an audience at the ABC studios in Hollywood (see admission ticket above right), but the production numbers were so elaborate and difficult that eventually the creators opted to tape the shows without an audience.

Julie termed her ambitious series "a wonderful challenge" and loved the idea of doing "fresh, new music every week." But she also admitted that it was exhausting to come up with a new hour of high-quality dance, music,

and comedy every week. When the series was finally canceled, she was in many ways relieved. Her final broadcast was a tribute to her old friend Henry Mancini, who whistled birdcalls during "Time Is My Friend," Julie's customary sign-off. This beautiful and thoughtful song was written by Julie herself, with lyricist Leslie Bricusse.

"Julie's Christmas Special" (ABC, December 14, 1973).
This holiday treat from London featured Peter Ustinov, Peggy Lee, and a magical winter setting. Julie sang "Hark, the Herald Angels Sing" and "Ring, Christmas Bells." Ustinov portrayed Santa Claus minus the red suit. Peggy Lee played the Sugar Plum Fairy and joined Julie in a medley of standards that included "Swinging on a Star," "Just in Time," and "Sentimental Journey."

"Julie on Sesame Street" (ABC, November 23, 1973).
Despite the logistical complications of re-creating the "Sesame Street" set, this charming special, pictured at right, was taped in London. The show featured a medley of songs with Perry Como and a montage of Broadway musical scenes with the Muppets. Julie sang "Bein' Green" with Kermit the Frog and closed the show with "What Do I Do When I'm Alone."

"*Julie and Jackie: 'How Sweet It Is'*" (ABC, May 22, 1974).
Jackie Gleason braved his first flight in twenty years to join Julie in London for a special celebrating his many television characters. As Sam the Bartender, he battled Eliza

Doolittle; as "Honeymooner" Ralph Kramden, he was paired with a new Norton (Julie). Gleason pantomimed "The Poor Soul" while Julie sang "You Gotta Have Heart," and the two danced to "Won't You Charleston with Me?" (pictured).

"*Julie and Dick in Covent Garden*" (ABC, April 21, 1974).
Dick Van Dyke and Carl Reiner were Julie's guests for this special, taped in London. A comic highlight of the show was their rendering of "Cinderella" in the style of a traditional

English pantomime. Here, Dick Van Dyke plays the Fairy Godmother to Julie's Cinderella. Van Dyke and Reiner also portrayed the ugly stepsisters, and with the help of trick editing, Julie managed to play opposite herself as the prince.

"*Julie 'My Favorite Things'*" (ABC, April 18, 1975).
Blake Edwards directed this musical celebration of Julie's personal favorites, including her daughter Emma in a cameo appearance on a unicycle, a Duke Ellington medley, a duet with Kermit the Frog, and a "ballet" with a troupe of Pink Panthers. The grand finale was a lavish spoof of Busby Berkeley movies, "Flying Down to Brighton," in which Peter Sellers played producer Binky Barclay.

"The Puzzle Children" (PBS, October 19, 1976). Public television featured Julie in this entertaining and informative look at children's learning disabilities. Bill Bixby did magic tricks, and Julie sang "Something," a new song by "Sesame Street" composer Joe Raposo.

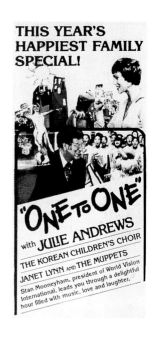

THIS YEAR'S HAPPIEST FAMILY SPECIAL!

"ONE to ONE"

with JULIE ANDREWS
THE KOREAN CHILDREN'S CHOIR
JANET LYNN and THE MUPPETS

Stan Mooneyham, president of World Vision International, leads you through a delightful hour filled with music, love and laughter.

"One to One" (syndicated, December 15, 1975).
This syndicated special was produced by World Vision International to promote the children's charity. Julie was teamed with the Korean Children's Choir for tunes such as "Getting to Know You," "I'd Like to Teach the World to Sing," "Day by Day," and "Do-Re-Mi."

"The Merv Griffin Show" (syndicated, December 26, 1975).
In this special tribute to director Robert Wise (at left), Julie recalled their two films together. She appeared occasionally on talk shows during the 1970s, most notably with David Frost and Dick Cavett.

"Salute to Sir Lew Grade—The Master Showman" (ABC, June 13, 1975).
This event, taped April 18 at the New York Hilton, honored Lew Grade, the storied English impresario responsible for "The Julie Andrews Hour" as well as many of her television specials. Julie's songs for the evening included "If," "Wouldn't It Be Loverly?," and "The Sound of Music." Tom Jones (pictured) joined her for a duet of "You Will Be My Music."

"The Muppet Show" (CBS, syndicated, 1978).
Julie was the guest star on an episode of Jim Henson's musical series. She sang "The Lonely Goatherd" from The Sound of Music with a chorus of Muppet dogs, chickens, and pigs, and she introduced one of her own songs, "When You Were a Tadpole and I Was a Fish," in a scene with Kermit the Frog.

"America Salutes the Queen" (NBC, November 29, 1977).
In Britain this variety special was titled the "Silver Jubilee Royal Variety Gala." It was taped November 21 at the London Palladium and included an impressive list of stars performing in honor of the Queen's Silver Jubilee. Here Julie is greeted backstage by Queen Elizabeth II and other members of the royal family. Bob Hope introduced Julie's segment of the show, which included a medley of "My Favorite Things," "Camelot," "I Could Have Danced All Night," and "The Sound of Music."

"Julie Andrews' Invitation to the Dance" (CBS, November 30, 1980). This "Festival of Lively Arts for Young People" was taped at the Merriwether Post Pavilion in Columbia, Maryland. The program illustrated the varieties of dance. Julie performed Cy Coleman's seductive "Anyone Can Do It" from Little Me *and "Shall We Dance?" Rudolf Nureyev sang and danced the seductive "I've Got Your Number" with Julie as his willing victim.*

"Julie Andrews: One Step into Spring" (CBS, March 9, 1978). For this CBS special, Julie sang "At the Ballet" from A Chorus Line *and a medley of "sexy" songs ("Fever," "A Good Man Is Hard to Find") with Leslie Uggams. Her other guest star, Miss Piggy, was chagrined to discover that she and Julie had identical bonnets for the Easter Parade (opposite).*

"The 38th Annual Tony Awards" (NBC, June 15, 1984). Julie and her Victor/Victoria *costar Robert Preston were cohosts for this annual Broadway awards show, which was broadcast live from the Gershwin Theatre in New York. In a special tribute to composer Stephen Sondheim (left), Julie sang a heartfelt rendition of his bittersweet "Send in the Clowns" from* A Little Night Music.*"*

"Mancini & Friends" (PBS, March 21, 1987). Henry Mancini's movie music was showcased in a "Great Performances" special (left) taped by KCET in Los Angeles. Julie sang "Whistling Away the Dark" and "Crazy World" accompanied by an orchestra conducted by Mancini himself. Here the entire cast poses with the honoree: (clockwise, from bottom left) Dudley Moore, Julie, Gary Owens, Steve Allen, Andy Williams, Sue Raney, Laurindo Almeida, and Johnny Mathis.

"AFI Salute to Jack Lemmon" (CBS, May 30, 1988).
The sixteenth annual American Film Institute Lifetime Achievement Award went to Jack Lemmon during a four-hour tribute on March 10, 1988. Julie was the gracious hostess for both the event and the one-hour CBS telecast honoring her friend and costar.

"Julie Andrews: The Sound of Christmas" (ABC, December 16, 1987).
Julie returned to Salzburg for a holiday special blessed with two talented costars, John Denver and Placido Domingo, and extraordinarily beautiful music and settings. The trio celebrated the Christmas season with a stirring waltz medley performed in the ornate Leopoldskron Castle. A highlight of the evening was Julie's soaring "Ave Maria" at the Church of Mondsee.

"*Julie and Carol Together Again*" (ABC, December 13, 1989).
Hollywood's historic Pantages Theater was the setting for a third TV special pairing Julie Andrews and Carol Burnett. The show was taped before an invited audience on June 9 and 10. Julie and Carol opened and closed the show with Stephen Sondheim's "Old Friends." Among the highlights of the evening: Julie singing and moonwalking Michael Jackson's "Bad" during a medley of 1970s and 1980s songs (left); and a friendly tea party erupting into an all-out food fight in which Carol squeezes a large cream donut into Julie's cleavage.

"*The 45th Annual Tony Awards*" (CBS, June 2, 1991).
Julie and Jeremy Irons cohosted this live event from the Minskoff Theatre in New York. During rehearsals, Julie asked Irons to sing with her in a tribute to her Broadway musicals, but he declined, explaining that "no one can beat Rex when it comes to that." The awards show featured Julie singing a nostalgic medley of "Wouldn't It Be Loverly?," "Camelot," and "I Could Have Danced All Night."

"*Christmas in Washington*" (NBC, December 19, 1992). Taped in the National Buildings Museum, this annual Christmas gala included songs from Julie's holiday repertoire, "Sunny Bank" and "The Holy Boy," as well as a pretty duet, "The Secret of Christmas," with Peabo Bryson. Here, Julie is joined in the grand finale ("Hark, the Herald Angels Sing") by Bryson (far left), First Lady Barbara Bush, Neil Diamond, President George Bush, and classical violinist Midori. The chorus is the U.S. Naval Academy Glee Club supplemented by the Soul Children of Chicago gospel choir.

*"Our Sons" (*ABC*, May 19, 1991).*
Julie made an auspicious movie-for-television debut as a wealthy widow and businesswoman who learns that her son's male lover is dying of AIDS. *Hugh Grant plays Julie's son; Zeljko Ivanek plays his lover. And as the estranged mother of the dying man, Ann-Margret was terrific as Julie's exact opposite, an uneducated, fearful woman who cannot forgive her son's homosexuality. The women come together, learning tolerance of one another and acceptance of their sons. This sensitive film, with strong performances by both actresses, was directed by John Erman. Below, the costars pose at the premiere, May 2, 1991, at the Directors' Guild Theater in West Hollywood. The event was a benefit for the Shanti Foundation, which provides support services to people with* HIV *infection and* AIDS.

"Julie" (ABC, May 30 to July 4, 1992).
Blake Edwards directed six episodes of this situation comedy, based on his 1991 pilot, "Millie," which has never been broadcast (see publicity photo, right). Julie portrays an actress who moves to Sioux City with her new husband, Sam (played by James Farentino, left). The fourth episode revolved around an orangutan, their unlikely houseguest. The series did not attract an audience and was dropped after the fifth episode.

"Julie Andrews . . . In Concert" (PBS, March 9, 1990).
This program was taped in August 1989 at the restored art deco Wiltern Theatre in Los Angeles, the last stop in Julie's cross-country concert tour. "Great Performances" produced this public television special, which was a fine representation of Julie's autobiographical evening. In recounting her life story, the repertoire included "London Pride," "Come Rain or Come Shine," and a pleasing Lerner and Lowe medley.

"Some Enchanted Evening: Celebrating Oscar Hammerstein II" (PBS, March 6, 1995). *Julie hosted this "Great Performances" tribute to America's favorite lyricist, opening the program with a thoughtful rendition of Rodgers and Hammerstein's "A Cock-Eyed Optimist" and finishing with an emotional performance of "Edelweiss," among the last lyrics written by Oscar Hammerstein.*

"Great Performances" has also produced "Julie Andrews: Back on Broadway." It debuted on PBS October 25, 1995.

5
People, Places, and Events

Julie is celebrated around the world for a remarkable career encompassing stage, film, television, recordings, and the concert stage. Among friends and family, she is also known (and celebrated) as a warm, sensitive, bright, upbeat, funny human being. She is a published author, a dedicated contributor to international charities, and an enthusiastic fan of fine art, theater, movies, literature, and both popular and classical music.

After nearly fifty years in the spotlight, Julie remains every inch the star. She is beloved by millions not merely because of her exceptional talent and remarkable beauty, but because she affirms life and humanity in everything she undertakes. And there's no sign that the pace of accomplishments will diminish. Her outlook: "I get so much pleasure out of what I do that I hope there will continue to be opportunities for me." In a recent interview, she noted, "Earlier on, I would perform in order to run away from myself and from my life. But these days, I really run to embrace it." On another occasion she said, "There's so much music I want to make, and there's such joy in it, and I feel I have so much to give still, that I'm just not ready to sit back."

Her two youngest children, Amy and Joanna, are just beginning college, she has embarked on her first Broadway show in more than thirty years (*Victor/Victoria*; see Chapter 6), and she entertains frequently on television and the concert stage. She also serves as a special goodwill ambassador for the United Nations Development Fund for Women and works tirelessly on behalf of Operation USA, Save the Children, and other favorite charities.

Julie and Tony Walton's daughter, Emma, is also the recipient of boundless time, love, and devotion from her mother (and father). Emma is currently artistic director of the highly respected Bay Street Theatre in Sag Harbor, Long Island, New York, where Julie frequently appears as an entertainer in special benefits for the company.

Julie and her husband, Blake Edwards, share a deep, loving, supportive relationship. A few weeks after the opening of their grandest, most ambitious collaboration—the Broadway adaptation of their hit movie *Victor/Victoria*—they celebrated twenty-six years of marriage. About Blake, Julie says, "I have noticed that as a director, husband, everything, he explores one step further than most other people I've ever met, and this makes him fascinating to me. I've learned to try not to close my mind to anything, to keep an open mind, to allow for new possibilities."

Summing it all up, Julie has said, "Ah, but I was unbelievably lucky. I've always said the same thing: luck and timing were on my side. I've been completely blessed with good fortune. In reality, I lead a charmed life!" This chapter highlights Julie Andrews's remarkable life, a life filled with interesting people, places, and events.

During the London run of My Fair Lady, *Julie married her childhood sweetheart, Anthony (Tony) Walton, in St. Mary's Church at Weybridge, Surrey, on May 10, 1959. Here, Ted Wells, Julie's father, leads her through a mob of fans and news photographers assembled in and around the church.*

Julie's My Fair Lady *costar, Stanley Holloway, congratulates the happy bride.*

Julie's white organza silk wedding gown was designed by Tony Walton, who has since gone on to become one of the most talented and respected stage designers on Broadway and in the West End.

Julie and Tony flew to San Francisco and Los Angeles for their honeymoon and a guest television appearance on a Jack Benny special. She returned to London and My Fair Lady on May 25 and remained in the show until August 8, 1959.

Julie wore her Camelot crown and a cast T-shirt to play the role of catcher for the Broadway Softball League, which was celebrating "Ralph Bellamy Day" in Central Park (April 20, 1961). Lucille Ball is at bat—she was starring in the Broadway musical *Wildcat*. The umpire is Joe E. Brown, who was playing Captain Andy in a revival of *Showboat*.

Julie and comedians Benny Hill, Arthur Askey, and Danny Kaye meet the Duke of Edinburgh backstage at the "Royal Midnight Matinee," a fund-raising event at the London Palladium (October 26, 1959).

Julie was 27 when Emma Kate Walton was born at the London Clinic on November 27, 1962. Here the doting parents share a very happy moment.

Julie and Tony's hectic work schedules often kept them apart for extended periods of time, and a difficult situation simply worsened when Julie rocketed to Hollywood stardom. This photo reflects their happiest time. After their divorce in May 1968, Julie told reporters: "When I married Tony, I thought it would last forever. Gosh, we had known each other since we were children. But he had his career and I had mine and we let ourselves drift apart."

191

Julie and her beautiful baby daughter. Julie made a point of spending as much time as possible with little Emma, who became a familiar face on her mother's movie sets.

Movie Life *magazine conjured up a "scandal" with this photograph of Julie, in costume for the wedding scene in* The Sound of Music. *Julie's extraordinary popularity made her a frequent topic for the Hollywood gossip-mongers.*

President Lyndon B. Johnson's inaugural gala featured an all-star lineup, including Mike Nichols (left, behind President Johnson), Barbra Streisand (partially obscured by Lady Bird), Julie, and Carol Burnett. Ann-Margret, Carol Channing, and Harry Belafonte were also featured performers that evening.

On February 8, 1965, Julie received her first Golden Globe Award as Best Motion Picture Actress in a Musical or Comedy (for Mary Poppins). The ceremony was telecast live on "The Andy Williams Show." Julie is seen here with Williams, presenters Tony Franciosa and Abbe Lane, and, on the right, "Miss Golden Globes." In her acceptance speech, Julie said: "I would like to thank particularly the man who made all this possible . . . Jack Warner." It was a pointed remark spurred by Warner's decision not to cast her in his movie version of My Fair Lady. Warner, who was sitting in the front row, took Julie's ribbing with good grace, referring to her later that evening as "what's her name?" At right, the old movie tycoon offers Julie a friendly buss.

On April 5, 1965, at the Santa Monica Civic Auditorium, Julie received the Best Actress award for her performance in Mary Poppins. *On the morning after she received the award (opposite page), Julie told reporters: "It's heavy, but I won't let it go." Rex Harrison, above, also received an Oscar that year for, irony of ironies,* My Fair Lady. *His movie costar, Audrey Hepburn, who had not been nominated, presented the award to Harrison, prompting a graceful thank-you: "Deep love to two fair ladies." At left, Audrey is seen congratulating Julie. Though the media had tried to depict them as bitter rivals, the two actually became very good friends.*

Soon after her Oscar and the phenomenal success of The Sound of Music, *Julie became the favorite cover girl of virtually every popular magazine of the day.*

Superstar Julie Andrews with friends and fellow celebrities:

With Roddy McDowall and Marcello Mastroianni at the Coconut Grove nightclub.

With Fred Astaire at a Hollywood ceremony.

With Barbra Streisand after a performance of Funny Girl.

With James Stewart after she received the "Star of the Year" award from the Theatre Owners of America (October 30, 1965).

With Julie Christie back-stage at the 1966 Academy Awards. Christie had just won the Best Actress award for Darling.

With presenters Gene Kelly and Barbara Stanwyck at the twenty-third Golden Globe Awards. Julie had just received the award for Best Actress for The Sound of Music *(January 31, 1966).*

With Sean Connery at the Whiskey-a-Go-Go discotheque.

With Mae West on the set of STAR!

With presenters Natalie Wood and Rock Hudson and "Favorite Actor" Steve McQueen at the twenty-fourth Golden Globe Awards (February 15, 1967). Julie was voted "World Film Favorite Actress" that year and received the honor again in 1968.

With Shirley MacLaine at a party for Edith Head.

The filming of Hawaii *(opposite) brought Julie to the islands for the first time. While in Honolulu, she attended a performance of the American Ballet Theatre and paid a personal visit to troops en route to Vietnam.*

Julie follows in the tradition of other great Hollywood stars at Grauman's Chinese Theatre, March 26, 1966. Always the comedian, she amused the huge crowd when her high heels became stuck in the cement.

Blake and Julie share a quiet moment on the set of Darling Lili. *Blake proposed to Julie over the phone after playing her a Henry Mancini tune.*

Julie and Blake were married in a private ceremony in her California garden on November 13, 1969. The children were in school at the time, so the service was videotaped, but when the tape turned out to be faulty, the wedding was "restaged," with considerable humor, for a second taping. Here, Blake and Julie are seen during their courtship on the set of Darling Lili.

During the making of Darling Lili, *Julie became better acquainted with Blake's children, daughter Jennifer and son Geoffrey. Following completion of the film, Julie took almost three years away from her career to devote herself wholly to her new family.*

While Julie was filming Darling Lili *on location in Ireland, her father, Ted Wells, visited her at the palatial Carlton House near Dublin. Julie has said, "When I was with him, everything was forgotten except the outdoor life."*

Julie with her "Mum," Barbara Andrews, who was visiting Los Angeles. About her mother Julie once said, "I am sure I got my love of music, singing, and dancing from her."

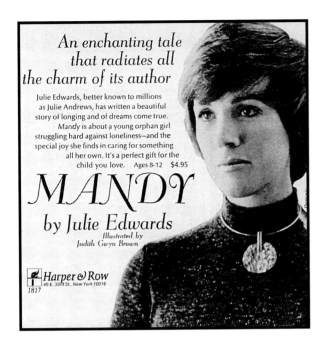

An enchanting tale
that radiates all
the charm of its author

Julie Edwards, better known to millions
as Julie Andrews, has written a beautiful
story of longing and of dreams come true.
Mandy is about a young orphan girl
struggling hard against loneliness—and the
special joy she finds in caring for something
all her own. It's a perfect gift for the
child you love.   Ages 8-12 $4.95

MANDY

by Julie Edwards

Illustrated by
Judith Gwyn Brown

Harper & Row
49 E. 33rd St., New York 10016
1817

Julie wrote her first children's book, Mandy, *after losing eleven-year-old Jennifer Edwards's challenge to stop swearing. This touching story of an orphan girl was published in 1971 and sweetly dedicated to Jenny.*

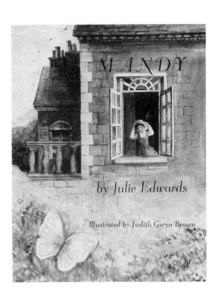

MANDY

by Julie Edwards

Illustrated by Judith Gwyn Brown

The Last of the
Really Great
Whangdoodles

JULIE EDWARDS

A delightful new fantasy by the
well-known, well-loved author

THE LAST OF
THE REALLY GREAT
WHANGDOODLES

by Julie Edwards

Three children set off on a magical odyssey to the amazing kingdom created by the last of the really great Whangdoodles. Lindy, Thomas and Benjamin must outwit astonishing creatures like Sidewinders, Tree Squeaks

and Swamp Gaboons before they meet the fabulous Whangdoodle and grant him his heart's desire. Julie (Andrews) Edwards is the author of the popular MANDY. Ages 8-12. $5.95 at bookstores

Harper & Row
10 E. 53rd St., New York 10022
1817

Julie published a second book, The Last of the Really Great Whangdoodles, *in 1974. She had discovered the word* whangdoodle *in the dictionary and was intrigued by its definition as a "humorous, mythical creature of fanciful and undefined*

nature." At the time of its publication, she said: "My new book was written for children, or perhaps I should say for the child in us all. It's about a wonderful creature who created for himself a fantastic kingdom of fun and happiness and beauty."

205

Although her television series, "The Julie Andrews Hour," was canceled after its first season, it was critically acclaimed and honored with seven Emmy Awards. The series is a treasure chest of superb musical numbers by its talented and hard-working star.

Julie rehearses with her good friend Andre Previn and the London Symphony Orchestra for a concert of Christmas carols at Royal Albert Hall, December 4, 1973.

Peter Sellers took these blissful pictures of Julie, Blake, and their newly adopted daughters Amy Leigh (left) and Joanna Lynn on the porch of the family's home in Switzerland. The Vietnamese orphans were lovingly embraced by the family that Julie has called "His, Mine, and Ours."

Julie visits Blake on the set of Wild Rovers. *She has said in a notable expression of love and admiration for Blake: "There are lots of other directors I'd like to work for—Blake and I are not bound at the hip. But, honestly, the most convenient and pleasant is the one right under my nose, my husband."*

With contemporary songs as well as old favorites, Julie created a concert act (opposite), which she first performed at the London Palladium in 1976. The act included most of her Broadway and Hollywood hits. Julie told reporters: "I want to take the audience on a sentimental jouney—for them and for me."

Blake's hit comedy, Return of the Pink Panther, *premiered in Gstaad, Switzerland, in 1975, with special guests Richard Burton and Elizabeth Taylor in attendance. Henry Mancini can be seen standing just behind Julie and Peter Sellers.*

Peter Sellers as Inspector Clouseau, and Julie as a hotel maid, on the set of Return of the Pink Panther. *Julie's comic cameo ended up on the cutting-room floor. However, fans of Blake's Pink Panther movies may want to take another look at* The Trail of the Pink Panther. *Could that be Julie dressed as a cleaning woman, observing the comic action in the hallway?*

Highlights of Julie's first concert act were a lively Charleston choreographed to the title tune from Thoroughly Modern Millie *and a tango set to "Baby Face" (above). The Las Vegas version of Julie's act premiered at Caesars Palace on August 12, 1976. She opened the show as a Buckingham Palace guard (right) and brought the audience to its feet with another production number, "One Piece at a Time," in which she dressed as an auto mechanic (opposite). It was her first and only Las Vegas engagement. After performing two shows per evening, at 9 and 12:30, for a limited run of one week, Julie was exhausted and decided it was an experience she didn't wish to repeat.*

What began as the "act" was soon shaped into a more sedate concert tour, minus the production numbers and dancers. Variations of this show were presented in Japan, Switzerland, Norway, and across the United States.

Julie's star on the Hollywood Walk of Fame is directly in front of the new addition to the Chinese Theatre. The star was dedicated on October 5, 1979, just after the Los Angeles City Council presented a resolution proclaiming "Julie Andrews Day." In her acceptance speech, she said: "I'm particularly thrilled that my star happens to be in front of a movie theater. I can only hope that millions and millions of feet will walk across that star and go right into the theater and see all the movies that are such a pleasure to make, and hopefully give you all so much pleasure, too."

On May 14, 1979, Julie joined Rex Harrison at the Winter Garden Theatre in New York for a one-night tribute to Lerner and Loewe titled A Very Special Evening. Her segment of the program included several songs from My Fair Lady, *a charming waltz with Rex Harrison, and an emotional rendition of "I Loved You Once in Silence," a song she had rarely performed since* Camelot.

In 1982 Julie traveled to Southeast Asia for twelve days, touring orphanages and hospitals on behalf of Operation California. She told a reporter, "It's one thing to speak about it from an intellectual point of view. I thought I ought to be able to speak personally. Going there would make what I had to say have more authority." She has been a fundraiser for the charity, now renamed Operation USA, since 1979.

On February 16, 1983, Julie was paraded around the Harvard campus before receiving the Hasty Pudding Award. A banner stretched across Massachusetts Avenue proclaimed "Jazz Hot Julie." In her acceptance speech, she said, "You gave Mary Poppins your highly esteemed award just to see if she sweats."

In 1983 Julie received her third Academy Award nomination, for Victor/Victoria. Looking every bit the superstar, she is seen here arriving for the ceremonies at the Dorothy Chandler Pavilion.

Julie with her daughter Emma at a 1983 American Cancer Society gala honoring Blake Edwards. Julie sang

Maury Yeston's "In a Very Unusual Way" (from the musical Nine*) as a tribute to her husband and their enduring relationship.*

Julie and her father, Ted Wells, in December 1984, after a memorial service for her mother, Barbara Andrews. At the service, held in St. Peter's Church, Surrey, Julie said: "She touched us and gave us joy and made the quality of our lives a little more special." About her father, who died in 1990, Julie said, "My father and I have always been very close. He is an open-air man who thought I should have a normal upbringing. He was never really in favor of show business, and he kept an eagle eye on things. Between the two worlds— my father's and my mother's—I really got a pretty good balance."

Julie with her five children in the mid-1980s: (clock-wise from left) Amy, Geoffrey, Emma, Jennifer, and Joanna.

Julie with four of her film directors: (from left) Robert Wise, George Roy Hill, Blake Edwards, and Arthur Hiller at a Women in Film tribute held in her honor on November 15, 1986.

On October 7, 1989, Julie received the British Academy of Film and Television Arts (BAFTA) Award from Princess Anne at the Odeon Leicester cinema in London. Millicent Martin, David Tomlinson, James Coburn, and James Fox spoke about their dear friend and costar, and filmed tributes came from Carol Channing, Dick Van Dyke, and James Garner. In a heartfelt acceptance, Julie said, "I am first and always English, and I carry my country in my heart wherever I go. I've tried to honor her, and I have the funny feeling that perhaps tonight, in some way, I've managed to do just that."

The Sound of Music *children were first reunited with Julie in 1973 (below) for the first reissue of the film. At the twenty-fifth anniversary celebration in 1990 (left), they came together again and posed for a similar photograph: (from left) Angela Cartwright, Charmian Carr, Kym Karath, Debbie Turner, Heather Menzies, and Duane Chase. (Nicholas Hammond was out of the country.) For the film's thirtieth anniversary in 1995, Julie hosted a special showing on network television.*

At the 1992 Cannes film festival, Blake Edwards was honored with a retrospective. Ten of his films were featured, and he premiered his director's cut of Darling Lili. *He surprised critics by cutting* almost *thirty minutes from the original release.*

Julie at a party in New York City with Leonard Bernstein and Kitty Carlisle Hart, the widow of Moss Hart, Julie's great Broadway mentor.

In 1992 Julie was named goodwill ambassador to the United Nations Development Fund for Women. One of her first duties included traveling to Loboudou, a tiny Senegalese village, where she presented local women with a grinding machine. UN activities have taken her to several other countries on similar missions.

On June 11, 1993, Julie received the Women in Film Crystal Award from Robert Wise. Her speech highlighted the great work of women in the film industry and included a special thanks to her husband (seen above). Reflecting on her career Julie has stated: "I think my whole body of work speaks for itself. I've had the most extraordinary chances."

6
Late Developments

After thirty-one years, Julie Andrews finally returned to the musical theater in New York. However, she did not choose to mark this momentous occasion with a starring role in a grand new Broadway show. Instead, in a typical display of humility and dedication to her craft, Julie opted to be one of five members of an ensemble cast in a small Off-Broadway revue called *Putting It Together*. Indeed, Julie admitted that the communal nature of the production, as well as its limited run of sixteen weeks, had initially drawn her to the project.

Julie's return to the stage, and the fact that the show featured an assembly of Stephen Sondheim songs, ensured that the Manhattan Theater Company production would be a success, but no one expected the public frenzy on that bitterly cold winter morning when the tickets went on sale. Thousands of people braved the bad weather, and the entire run was sold out in six hours.

Ironically, the only complaint of critics and lucky ticket-holders was that the show did not feature enough of Julie—the very thing she had chosen to avoid. People wanted to hear Julie sing and to see her shape a role. They wanted her to be the star, not just a face in the crowd.

Putting It Together proved to be excellent preparation for the theatrical adaptation of Blake and Julie's 1982 movie hit, *Victor/Victoria*. A stage production of the film had been in the planning for more than ten years, but a number of misfortunes, including the untimely death of Robert Preston, kept the show on the drawing board.

Finally, in the spring of 1995, the stage version of *Victor/Victoria* was Broadway-bound. It was a bittersweet moment for Julie and Blake, because Henry Mancini, their old friend and collaborator, the composer of *Victor/Victoria*, had died a few weeks before the first press conference announcing the show.

Victor/Victoria headed first to the heartland, to Minneapolis and Chicago, where it previewed to sell-out crowds and encouraging reviews. Finally, on October 25, 1995, at the Marquis Theatre on Times Square, Julie Andrews made her return to Broadway. Those who witnessed that opening night will never forget the rapturous cheers that greeted Julie's curtain call. It was a homecoming. It was a triumph!

From her earliest years as a child performer in England, nearly fifty years ago, the stage has been the foundation from which Julie created a rich and phenomenal career as an entertainer. She was blessed with a beautiful face, a magnificent voice, a gift for dance and comedy, and an outsize talent for connecting with the audience.

Julie was a headliner in the music halls of Great Britain during vaudeville's final days. She was at the very center of the golden age of musical theater on Broadway. She was a pioneer of variety shows and musical comedy on television. And she was a Hollywood superstar in the last glory days of the movie musical. Now, she's back on Broadway and better than ever.

Julie has said that entertaining is what she knows best, and that it has contributed to her definition of self. She is, in fact, the last in a line of great twentieth-century troupers—from Al Jolson to Fanny Brice, from Judy Garland to Fred Astaire. Julie Andrews has always been, and will always be, a star!

Julie and the other four members of Putting It Together *rehearse in a loft in Chelsea: (from left) Christopher Durang, Rachel York, Stephen Collins, and Michael Rupert. The revue was originally mounted in London in 1992 with an English cast.*

The company at an RCA recording session: (from left) Christopher Durang, Stephen Collins, musical director Scott Frankel, Rachel York, producer Cameron Mackintosh, composer-lyricist Stephen Sondheim, Michael Rupert, and record producer Jay David Saks.

Sondheim
PUTTING IT TOGETHER

Putting It Together *was a brilliant revue of Stephen Sondheim's theater songs, strung together by the composer under the loose premise of party encounters and dark revelations. Costumed in a silky blue jumpsuit, Julie portrayed a nameless sophisticate at a penthouse party. She performed songs of rage and pain with a thrilling combination of icy reserve and pathos. Julie told reporters: "The lady I play covers her pain with a lot of wit."*

Her perfectly enunci-ated rapid-fire rendition of "Getting Married Today," the lament of a frazzled bride-to-be, was one of the highlights of the evening. Stephen Sondheim remarked about Julie that "She's an extremely versatile actress who has a lovely, warm presence on the stage." She returned the compli-ment: "Stephen Sondheim is the reason I'm doing this."

Putting It Together *opened on April 1, 1993, at the Manhattan Theater Club, and played until May 23. The opening night party was held at "21."*

By the time the show debuted on Broadway on October 25, 1995, it was a tight, energetic, old-fashioned knock-'em-dead musical comedy.

Julie Andrews was the life force of Victor/Victoria. Her command of the stage, her impeccable timing, her remarkable voice were a welcome sight on Broadway. Among the highlights: a hilarious tango (above) with Rachel York as Norma, the Chicago moll; a poignant Chaplinesque rendering of "Crazy World"; and a thrilling "belt" performance of a luscious new ballad, "Living in the

Shadows," written by Leslie Bricusse and his new musical partner Frank Wildhorn. Tony Roberts (opposite) was a stand-out in the Robert Preston role of Toddy, and Michael Nouri made a handsome King Marchan (left).

While writing the film version of Victor/Victoria, Blake Edwards noted that it would make an excellent stage musical. Once the film was a hit, he initiated plans for a Broadway production, and more than a decade later, his dream of a Broadway show—Blake's first—became reality.

Julie, who had often lamented the "gloom and doom" of such modern musicals as Les Miserables and The Phantom of the Opera, told reporters, "I'm looking forward to giving people real pleasure."

The world premiere of Victor/Victoria was held at the historic Orpheum Theatre in Minneapolis (opposite) on May 23, 1995. The production, with its high comedy and colorful costumes and sets, dazzled Minneapolis audiences, despite the fact that the show was nearly three hours long.

Scenes and songs were dropped that summer during the Chicago run at the Shubert Theatre.

7
Recordings

Starlight Roof 1947 Columbia

Julie's first recording was the "Polonaise" from *Mignon*, presented in a two-record 78 RPM version of *Starlight Roof*, the West End revue that made her a child star. Vic Oliver introduces and chats with a twelve-year-old Julie before she sings the aria that thrilled theater audiences. As with all of the early British issues, this recording has never been released on compact disc.

"Je Veux Vivre"/"Come to the Fair" 1948 Columbia

This British 78 RPM single presents the famous waltz from Gounod's *Romeo and Juliet* ("Je Veux Vivre") as well as a traditional English air, "Come to the Fair." The latter is a charming duet with her stepfather, Ted Andrews, with piano accompaniment by her mother, Barbara.

"Ah! Vous Dirai—Je Mama"/"The Wren"
1948 Columbia

Julie sings Mozart and demonstrates her childhood virtuosity on this remarkable British 78 RPM single recording, which features Barbara Andrews on the piano and Ted Andrews conducting the orchestra.

Jack and the Beanstalk 1950 His Master's Voice

The British radio cast of "Educating Archie" recorded this 12-inch 78 RPM record, offering a comical version of the fairy tale. On side two, young Julie has an amusing dialogue with the puppet, Archie Andrews, culminating with a song, "When We Grow Up."

The Boy Friend 1955 RCA

Recorded on October 10, 1954, Julie's first album was released as a long-playing (LP) record in 1955. The exuberance of the original Broadway cast is captured on this crisp, monophonic recording, which includes "A Room in Bloomsbury" and "I Could Be Happy with You." This album was also released as a set of 45 RPM records and is now available on CD.

High Tor 1956 Decca

The music from this TV special was released as an LP record at the time of the broadcast. "High Tor" featured Julie as Bing Crosby's young costar. Her songs included "Once upon a Long Ago," "Sad Is the Life of the Sailor's Wife," and "When You're in Love." MCA, the company that owns the vintage Decca recordings, has yet to issue the musical on CD.

My Fair Lady 1956 Columbia

The original Broadway cast recorded this classic musical on March 24, 1956. The LP became *Billboard* magazine's number one bestseller for fifteen weeks and still holds a record 292 weeks as a Top 40 album. Julie's songs include "Show Me," "I Could Have Danced All Night," and "Just You Wait." *My Fair Lady* is available on CD, as well as on a special edition "Gold CD" which includes a recording-studio conversation among the performers.

Cinderella 1957 Columbia

The original television cast recorded *Cinderella* on March 19, 1957, just prior to the live telecast. This album, issued in stereo (a new technology at the time), featured Julie singing such Rodgers and Hammerstein favorites as "In My Own Little Corner," "Impossible, It's Possible," and "Ten Minutes Ago." The recording is available on CD.

Tell It Again 1957 Angel

Subtitled *Songs of Sense and Nonsense*, this collection of nursery rhymes, learning songs, puzzles, riddles, and lullabies was recorded with Gilbert and Sullivan star Martyn Green. The lively flute and percussion accompaniment is noteworthy, and listeners of all ages can appreciate Julie's rhythmic renditions of "Mary Had a Little Lamb," "Pussy-Cat," "Star Light Star Bright," and other children's favorites. The recording was released in monophonic sound and has never been reissued on CD.

The Lass with a Delicate Air 1957 RCA

Julie's first solo album was arranged by Irwin Kostal. She was so young-looking, he said "that she had trouble hailing a taxi, and she walked to the session in the pouring rain." This twelve-song collection of her favorites includes such British folk songs as "Canterbury Fair" and "Where'er You Walk." The latter was an important part of her childhood repertoire with her stepfather. A stereo edition was released in 1958, but the album has not been reissued on CD.

Julie Andrews Sings 1958 RCA

For her second album with Irwin Kostal, Julie selected such vibrant Broadway tunes as "I'm Old Fashioned," "Little Old Lady," and "It Might as Well Be Spring." RCA has yet to release this lovely stereophonic album on CD.

Rose-Marie 1958 RCA

A studio cast was selected to record this famous operetta in London in July 1958. Giorgio Tozzi was paired with Julie for "Indian Love Call." Julie's outstanding songs include "Door of My Dreams," "Minuet of the Minute," and "Pretty Things." A CD of this RCA "Living Stereo" recording has not been released.

My Fair Lady 1959 Columbia

The show was rerecorded by the London cast on February 1, 1959, to take advantage of the brand-new stereo process. The song selection remains the same, but the performers, having lived their roles for almost three years, seem to have varied and deepened their performances. The 1959 London cast version of *My Fair Lady* is available on CD.

"Tom Pillibi"/"Lazy Afternoon" 1960 London

This rare 45 RPM record single presents two interesting songs which have never been included on any of Julie's composite albums or CDs.

Camelot 1960 Columbia

Recorded immediately after its premiere, this cast album includes two exciting songs, "Take Me to the Fair" and "Fie on Goodness!," which were later cut from the stage show. Julie's personal contributions to the recording include "The Lusty Month of May," "I Loved You Once in Silence," and her delightful duet with Richard Burton, "What Do Simple Folk Do?" Her stage reprises of "Camelot" and "The Jousts" were not recorded. It is noteworthy that this original cast album ranked among the Top 40 albums for 151 weeks. It is available on CD.

Broadway's Fair Julie 1961 Columbia

A collection of twelve Broadway show tunes recorded in June 1961 with Henri Rene and his orchestra, the album features "I Feel Pretty," "This Is New," and "How Are Things in Glocca Morra?" Individual selections from this album have been reissued under several titles—e.g., seven of the songs, plus a previously unreleased "I'll Follow My Secret Heart," can be found in a CD called *Julie Andrews: A Little Bit of Broadway*. The original album has never been issued on CD.

Don't Go in the Lion's Cage Tonight 1962 Columbia

Robert Mersey arranged these vaudeville-style songs, including "Waiting at the Church," "I Don't Care," and "Alexander's Ragtime Band." A barber shop quartet backs several of the selections. Reissues of selected songs from *Don't Go in the Lion's Cage Tonight* have been released under various titles, and some of the songs are included in two of her CDs: *Julie Andrews: A Little Bit of Broadway* and *Best of Julie Andrews*. This unique collection of songs has never been issued in its entirety on CD.

Julie and Carol at Carnegie Hall 1962 Columbia

The soundtrack of this memorable television special with Carol Burnett was actually recorded with an audience prior to the taping of the show. Though the performances are slightly different, the material is identical and serves as a satisfying reminder of the legendary telecast. Highlights include Julie and Carol's marvel of a medley, "History of Musical Comedy," and Julie's exquisite solo performance of "Oh Dear, What Can the Matter Be." *Julie and Carol at Carnegie Hall* was rereleased on CD but is no longer available in that format.

"He Loves Me"/"Dear Friend" 1964 Columbia

The celebrated soprano solo, "Dear Friends," from the musical *She Loves Me*, was recorded by Julie for a British 45 RPM single, but has never been included in any of her composite albums or CDs.

Mary Poppins 1964 Buena Vista

This movie soundtrack album was a number one seller for fourteen weeks and earned Julie a Grammy Award for Best Children's Recording. Among the timeless melodies featured on the album: "Chim Chim Cheree," "Stay Awake," and "Feed the Birds." The album has been released on CD and includes comments and demo recordings by the composers.

The Sound of Music 1965 RCA

This soundtrack went gold two weeks after its release and was on the *Billboard* bestseller charts for 161 weeks. A special CD version of the soundtrack, with additional songs never before issued, is included with the laser disc version of this Rodgers and Hammerstein classic. RCA has also issued a CD comprising songs from the original soundtrack album rearranged in the order in which they appear in the film.

Your Favorite Christmas Music, Volume 4
1965 Firestone

In 1965, customers at Firestone tire stores could purchase this special LP recording for one dollar. It featured Julie and the Young Americans performing holiday selections arranged by Irwin Kostal. Julie sings "The Christmas Song," "Rocking," and "The Bells of Christmas." The album was available only during the season of its release and has never been reissued on CD.

Thoroughly Modern Millie 1967 Decca

This joyous soundtrack went gold in less than four weeks. The gatefold album includes several pages of color photographs from the film. In addition to the rollicking title tune, Julie sings such standards as "Baby Face" and "Poor Butterfly." *Thoroughly Modern Millie* is available on CD.

A Christmas Treasure 1967 RCA

Julie's first commercially released Christmas album was recorded in the summer of 1966 and initially issued in Firestone stores as *Christmas Volume 5*. The following year, RCA issued the album as *A Christmas Treasure*. It offered the same eleven cuts, selections such as "Joy to the World" and "Jingle Bells," plus one new song, "The Lamb of God," all richly orchestrated by Andre Previn. This popular album has been reissued often through the decades and is now available on CD.

STAR! 1968 20th Century Fox

This soundtrack album was exceptionally popular despite the film's poor showing at the box office. It's not surprising—the album presented Julie singing fourteen wonderful songs, including such standards as "Someone to Watch Over Me," "My Ship," and "Limehouse Blues." When the album was released as a CD, it included an extended version of the title song, previously available only on a 45 RPM record.

Darling Lili 1970 RCA

Though the songs in this album were not taken directly from the film's soundtrack, the lush Henry Mancini arrangements are very similar to the movie renditions. Julie's songs include "Whistling away the Dark," "Smile Away Each Rainy Day," and "I'll Give You Three Guesses," which is performed in two surprisingly different ways. *Darling Lili* has not been released on CD.

Julie and Carol at Lincoln Center 1971 Columbia

This soundtrack of Julie and Carol Burnett's second television special features "Wait Till the Sun Shines, Nellie" and a delightful medley of sixties songs ("Downtown," "Born Free," "Spinning Wheel"). Especially memorable is Julie's haunting solo performance of "He's Gone Away." The album has yet to be released on CD.

The Secret of Christmas 1975 Columbia

Arranged by Ian Frasier, *The Secret of Christmas* was Julie's second Christmas collection. Comprising twelve holiday carols, the album was originally released in England, where it received glowing reviews. An early 1960s recording of "Silent Night," as well as a new song, "Secret of Christmas," were added to the mix when the album was issued in the United States in 1982. The complete version, offering such songs as "What Child Is This?," "Patapan," and "In the Bleak Midwinter," is available on CD under a new title, *Christmas with Julie Andrews*.

The Pink Panther Strikes Again 1976 United Artists

This movie soundtrack album features Julie singing a Mancini song, "Until You Love Me," in a deep, disguised alto. The voice is credited to Ainsley Jarvis, and the track was used in the movie as the voice of a drag entertainer. *The Pink Panther Strikes Again* has not been released on CD.

An Evening with Julie Andrews 1977 RCA

This Japanese release, representing Julie's only live concert album, was recorded during her triumphant September 21, 1977, concert at the Osaka Festival Hall in Japan. *An Evening with Julie Andrews* is a stellar representation of Julie's earlier concert performances. It features such favorites as Sondheim's "Being Alive," "I'd Rather Leave While I'm In Love" and a terrific medley of her Broadway and movie hits. RCA has yet to issue this album as a CD.

"10" 1979 Warner Bros.

This movie soundtrack includes Julie's solo, "He Pleases Me," and a duet with Dudley Moore, "It's Easy to Say." A single release from the film, Ravel's "Bolero," was a popular hit at the time. The album has not been released on CD.

Victor/Victoria 1982 MGM

This superb Henry Mancini soundtrack was originally released in a deluxe gatefold album. "Le Jazz Hot," "Crazy World," and Julie's loving duet with Robert Preston, "You and Me," are included on the album. The soundtrack has also been issued as a CD, with added instrumental selections and Robert Preston's drag performance of "Shady Dame from Seville."

Love Me Tender 1983 Peach River (Runaway)

Julie went to Nashville in 1978 to record this unusual collection of "middle of the road" pop songs. The album was first released in England with fourteen songs, including "You Don't Bring Me Flowers," "Crazy," "Another Somebody Done Somebody Wrong Song," and the classic title song, with Johnny Cash contributing vocal support. Although the American release offered only ten of the cuts, a Japanese issue features sixteen songs, adding "We Don't Make Love Anymore" and "I Still Miss Someone." This unique album has never been released on CD.

Love, Julie 1987 USA

This jazz-style album was originally recorded by Julie as a special birthday gift for her husband, Blake Edwards, who then suggested its commercial release. *Love, Julie*, created in collaboration with arranger-musical director Bob Florence, includes "My Lucky Day," "How Deep Is the Ocean," "Come Rain or Come Shine," and nine other selections. An extended version of Florence's original piece, "A Soundsketch," can be heard in the cut entitled "Jewels" on his own album called *Trash Can City*. Both albums are available on CD.

"The Sound of Christmas"/"O Come All Ye Faithful"
1987 USA
Though both songs are featured on other Julie Andrews holiday albums, this 45 RPM single rendition offers entirely new arrangements and recordings of these classic Christmas favorites. Ian Frasier, a longtime associate of Julie's, produced this rich and expressive version of "Faithful" with full choral backup. These arrangements have never been included in any of Julie's holiday CD releases.

The Sounds of Christmas—From Around the World
1990 Hallmark
Julie was Hallmark's first choice for the company's 1990 holiday offering. The album was recorded in London in April 1989 and includes "Have Yourself a Merry Little Christmas," "Sleigh Ride," "Ding Dong Merrily on High," a medley of European lullabies, and six other unusual carols. This limited edition CD and tape cassette were available for sale exclusively to customers making other purchases in Hallmark stores.

The King and I 1992 Philips
This special studio cast recording utilized the same thrilling orchestrations as those created for the 1956 film version of the Rodgers and Hammerstein classic. Julie sings Anna, Ben Kingsley portrays the King, and Lea Salonga (*Miss Saigon*) and Peabo Bryson sing the roles of Tuptim and Lun Tha. John Mauceri and the Hollywood Bowl Orchestra accompany such favorites as "Getting to Know You," "Whistle a Happy Tune," and "Shall We Dance." Dialogue from the show is sprinkled throughout the recording to add the flavor of the original musical drama. *The King and I* was released on both CD and tape cassette. At the time of its release vinyl versions were also available in Europe.

Putting It Together 1993 RCA
With Stephen Sondheim personally supervising the recording sessions, this cast album was recorded over a period of several days during the revue's limited Off-Broadway run. Julie's memorable contributions to both the show and the album include "Could I Leave You?," "Getting Married Today," and "Like It Was." This album was issued on both CD and tape cassette.

Julie Andrews: Broadway—The Music of Richard Rodgers 1994 Philips
In the first of a composers series, Julie sings many Richard Rodgers standards, including "Bewitched," "I Have Dreamed," and a beautiful medley of Rodgers waltzes. Another of the album's highlights is a moving rendition of "Edelweiss." This album was released on both CD and tape cassette. Julie's next Philips album will cover the music of Lerner and Loewe.

Acknowledgments

The authors gratefully acknowledge assistance from the following individuals and organizations:

Dan Woodruff and Robert Cushman, the Motion Picture Academy Library, Los Angeles; Cliff Carson, photo restoration, Los Angeles; Black and Color Lab, Hollywood; Karen LeGault, office/computer assistance, Los Angeles; Judy Chesterman, photo research, London; Bill Clem and Peter Cromarty, Peter Cromarty Associates, New York; Bill O'Donnell, WNET/Great Performances, New York; and Sylvia Clay, Janet Dubin, T. J. Edwards, Mrs. Larry Ford, Richard Giammanco, Phyllis Marcotte, Sandy Mangino, Les Perkins, John Sala, Barry Santiago, Dan Smith, Ginger Thompson, Marie-Jeanne van Hovell, Greg Vic, and Scott Wolf.

Very special thanks to Susan Marchand, for photo research and permissions; Jennifer Warner, for editorial assistance; Nancy Crossman, Kim Bartko, Dawn Barker, and the staff of Contemporary Books for their professionalism and patience; and Tony Adams, Jac Venza, David Horn, and Glenn DuBose for their essential encouragement and support.

This book is the beautiful byproduct of a 1995 PBS television tribute, "Julie Andrews: Back on Broadway," produced by WNET/New York for Great Performances.

Photo Credits

© Copyright Academy of Motion Picture Arts and Sciences: pp. 195, top; 198, bottom right; 213, top right.

Courtesy of the Academy of Motion Picture Arts and Sciences: pp. 90, bottom left; 98, bottom left; 137, bottom left; 137, bottom right; 162, top; 167, top.

Aquarius U.K.: pp. 10, bottom; 31; 32, top right.

Photo, Lisa Berg: p. 180, bottom.

Billy Rose Theatre Collection, The New York Public Library for the Performing Arts, Astor, Lenox, Tilden Foundation: pp. vii; 40; 42, bottom left; 47, top; 48–49; 51, bottom; 52; 55, top; 55, bottom; 56–57; 58, bottom; 59; 128, bottom; 130, top left; 130, top right; 130, bottom.

Courtesy Ethel Buchanan: pp. xviii; 4.

CBS: pp. 150; 151, left; 152, bottom; 153, top; 154, bottom.

Courtesy Alexander Cohen: p. 174, bottom.

Howell Conant, *Life* magazine, © Time, Inc.: p. 196, top.

Globe: pp. x; 50; 60, bottom; 68, top; 68, bottom; 89; 104, top; 105, bottom; 105, top; 127; 131, bottom left; 132, bottom right; 133, top; 136, bottom left; 138, top left; 139, top right; 140, top right; 142, top right; 144; 152, top; 156, top; 161, top; 161, bottom; 163, top; 164, bottom left; 165; 180, top; 191, top; 191, bottom; 194; 199, bottom right; 202, bottom; 204, bottom; 206, bottom; 207, top; 207, bottom; 213, top left; 214, top left; 216, center right; 216, bottom; 217, top.

Courtesy of Harvard News Office: p. 213, bottom left.

Courtesy Mr. Jon Holliday: pp. 32, top left; 32, bottom.

Photo, Polly Howard: pp. 210, bottom; 211, bottom left.

Hulton Deutsch Collection: p. 21.

Photo, Joan Marcus: pp. 142, bottom left; 222, top; 222, bottom; 223; 226.

Photograph by Angus McBean, Theatre Museum, V & A: p. 24, top.

Photo, Roddy McDowall: p. xi.

Museum of the City of New York: pp. 36; 41; 42, top; 43, top.

Neal Peters Collection: pp. 54; 159, bottom; 160, bottom; 167, bottom; 211, bottom right; 230.

Photo, Terry Nelson: p. 139, bottom right.

Photo, Don Perdue: p. 183, top; 183, bottom.

Photofest: pp. 11, top; 128, top left; 128, center left; 128, center right; 131, top left; 131, top right; 140, top left; 141, bottom; 147; 148, bottom; 149; 184; 228.

Photo © 1995 Carol Rosegg/Joan Marcus: pp. 142, center right; 142, bottom right; 218; 224, top; 224, bottom; 225, top; 225, bottom.

Photo, Greg Vie: pp. 142, top left; 181, bottom.

© 1996 Time, Inc. Reprinted by permission: p. 196, center left.

Other illustrations and photographs are from private collections.